The Art of Legislative Politics

State capitol, Madison, Wisconsin

The Art of Legislative Politics

Tom Loftus

A Division of Congressional Quarterly Inc.
Washington, D.C.

Photo credits:
Assembly Democratic Caucus: 4, 8, 9, 11
Legislative Reference Bureau: 5, 6
Personal collection: 1, 2, 7, 10, 12
Craig Schreiner, ii
Sun Prairie *Star:* 3

The quote attributed to Bob Vanasek on pages 37-38 is from a panel discussion during the State of the States Symposium, December 14, 1989, Eagleton Institute of Politics, Rutgers University.

Copyright © 1994 Congressional Quarterly Inc.
1414 22nd Street, N.W., Washington, D.C. 20037

Cover design by Debra Naylor.

Printed and bound in the United States of America.

Library of Congress Cataloging-in-Publication Data
Loftus, Tom, 1945-
    The art of legislative politics / Tom Loftus.
    p. cm.
    Includes bibliographical references and index.
    ISBN 0-87187-981-6 (hard) : ISBN 0-87187-980-8 (soft)
    1. Legislative bodies--United States--States. 2. State
governments--United States. 3. Wisconsin. Legislature. I. Title.
JK2488.L64 1994
320.9775'09'048--dc20   94-19620
                                                              CIP

*To the late Harvey Dueholm,
member of the Wisconsin Assembly from 1958 to 1978.
A wise and humorous man, so honest in his public sayings
that a state building has yet to be named after him.*

Contents

Foreword

This is an unusual book about an important subject written by a rare politician.

The state legislature is the subject. Since the late 1960s when I began observing them, state legislatures have modernized and strengthened themselves. They have insisted on sharing in policy making, budgeting, and even administration with governors and the executive branch. They have enthusiastically taken on the responsibility and begun exercising the power devolved upon them by the federal government. The states, and state legislatures, are where the action is today.

I have been writing about state legislatures for some time. Other political scientists have made their contributions to the literature. So, what is special about this book by Tom Loftus? What is special is the perspective and insight he brings to the subject. His insider's knowledge, a product of fourteen years in the Wisconsin Assembly, is what distinguishes *The Art of Legislative Politics* from what political scientists have done.

Over the years, few legislators have reflected in print about their experiences in the legislative process. They could not do it while they were still "in" and they did not do it after they were "out." One notable exception was Frank Smallwood, who was elected to the Vermont Senate while on leave from teaching political science at Dartmouth. His record of a two-year term, *Free and Independent*, published in 1976, was a gem. But, alas, it has been out of print for a while. Loftus's account fills the vacuum splendidly.

The Vermont Legislature, in which Smallwood served, is unlike any other legislative body in the nation. So is the Wisconsin legislature where Loftus distinguished himself. Indeed, all legislatures differ from one another as do all states. Yet, as I have discovered, to know one legislature is to know others as well. This rich exploration of the legislative process in Wisconsin specifically is a good way to understand the legislative process generally.

Legislatures are complex and subtle, constantly being shaped and reshaped by people, politics, and circumstances. They do not stand still; they are not easy to grasp. The next best thing to serving in the legislature is to observe legislative life one step removed, through someone as bright, incisive, candid, and witty as Tom Loftus. He tells it like it is, perhaps with an extra measure of humor. I believe that if Garrison Keillor of Lake Wobegone, Minnesota, were writing about the legislature, it would read like this book by Tom Loftus of Sun Prairie, Wisconsin.

Loftus is an admirable individual and was an outstanding legislator; that is one reason why this is a wonderful book. While in office, Loftus demonstrated genuine respect and affection for the legislature as an institution of representative democracy. His positive attitude is evident throughout these pages. Although he was not an apologist for everything that went on under the capitol dome, he would never undermine or bash the institution, as so many incumbents do these days. Cynicism is simply not in his nature, nor does it color the picture of the legislature you will read about in this book.

His colleagues in the Assembly quickly recognized his character and skill. That is why he was elected Democratic majority leader after just four years of service and why he was elected Speaker two years later—and then was reelected for three additional terms. Ability counts in Wisconsin, as it does in just about every legislature.

A man of principle, Loftus was also a pragmatic leader. That is evident in his discussion of strategies and tactics in the chapters that follow. In his political dealings, he showed friendship and respect toward his colleagues, even those who disagreed with him on the issues. A liberal himself, he was popular with lawmakers on the right as well as on the left. The Democratic caucus, which split into several factions, appeared to be unmanageable, but Loftus managed it nonetheless. And despite increasing partisanship in the Wisconsin legislature, he knew how to work with the minority Republicans. To accomplish things for the people of Wisconsin, he would have to compromise; and when he had to, he did.

In 1990 Loftus left the legislature to run for governor. The uphill race, in which he challenged Republican governor Tommy Thompson, did not go well for him. It was not a trouncing, but it was not a close race either. Leaving the legislature is tough enough, but losing a statewide election makes one's exit from public life doubly difficult. Most politicians need time to lick their wounds and to shake off their withdrawal symptoms. They have trouble moving on and adapting to another life. But not Loftus. The support he got from his family and his confidence in his own ability to be productive in other fields made the transition a happy one for him.

In the spring of 1991, Loftus, his wife, Barbara, and their sons, Alec and Karl, moved to Cambridge, Massachusetts for a semester, where he had been awarded a fellowship at the Institute of Politics at the John F. Kennedy School of Government. He had once taught part-time at the University of Wisconsin at Whitewater, so he was not a stranger to university life. He adapted instantly to Harvard, donning appropriate attire (brown corduroy pants and a heather green crewneck sweater), auditing a course on Shakespeare, and showing up religiously for the Tuesday and Wednesday dinners and Thursday lunches at the institute. Advising students to check their sacred cows at the door, Loftus led a weekly study group, "Government Is Part of the Solution." His optimism was undiminished.

It is not unheard of for state legislators to make their way to Harvard or to the University of Wisconsin (where Loftus worked when he returned home). Nor is it surprising to see former legislators in the U.S. Congress or in statewide office. But I cannot think of any former state legislator who received a presidential appointment as ambassador, as did Loftus. On first thought, it is difficult to conceive of a state legislator in the statesmanlike role of Ambassador to Norway, even one from Wisconsin and of Norwegian heritage. (I had always been told that a statesman was a dead politician, not a live one.) On second thought, although Loftus may not be in the mold of the career foreign service officer or that of the fat-cat political contributor, he is ideal ambassadorial timber. President Clinton could not have made a better choice.

The United States is fortunate to have such a skilled politician as Tom Loftus representing its interests in Oslo. And Norway is fortunate to be visited by his wit and charm. And all of us at home are lucky that, between careers, Loftus has found time to write this marvelous book.

Alan Rosenthal
Eagleton Institute of Politics
Rutgers University

Acknowledgments

The idea of writing this book took hold after my unsuccessful campaign for governor of Wisconsin in 1990. Leaving the legislature after fourteen years was not difficult. I wanted to go. But what then? Thanks to the Institute of Politics at the John F. Kennedy School of Government at Harvard University, I didn't have to think a lot about that question. I was asked to be an IOP fellow for one semester. It was a glorious spring semester that gave me time to think and my family a rest from political life.

I left Cambridge with an outline for a book. That was the seed. But the nurturing of the project was by Professor Alan Rosenthal of the Eagleton Institute of Politics at Rutgers University. Alan urged me on, said nothing when he disliked a draft of a chapter, and heaped praise when he read one he liked. The book's other midwife was Madison attorney and friend Brady Williamson. His wise counsel, and his assumption that good things happen to those who forge ahead, are reflected in this project. A special thanks to the Evjue Foundation of Madison, Wisconsin, and the Kohl Foundation of Milwaukee for some early financial help.

And, thanks to those friends who read the draft—Neil Shively, Nan Cheney, Anne Arnesen, Hal Bergan—all of them made a contribution. There was also an angel of help at all times, and that is Sue Meyer, who has been a trusted aide in everything I have undertaken since she walked into my office in 1979. Finally, and most importantly, the biggest thanks goes to my wife Barbara, my partner in politics and everything else in life, and our children, Alec and Karl.

State Rep. David O'Malley tipped me off that he
would retire and not run for reelection.

With Barbara at campaign headquarters on
the night I won the 1976 Democratic nomination for Assembly.

Campaigning on a farm in Deerfield.

This portrait of "Fighting Bob" La Follette hangs in the
Wisconsin Speaker's office.

Pictured here in 1982, state Rep. Tom Hauke survived an ethics scandal and was easily reelected.

On the floor of the Assembly with Representatives Dismas Becker and Midge Miller during my first session.

A successful lobbyist and former state senator, Gary Goyke, pictured here in 1979, raised more than a few eyebrows with his lobbying methods.

Gov. Lee Sherman Dreyfus signs the budget bill as I look on with (from left) Assembly Minority Leader Tommy Thompson, Senate Minority Leader Walter Chilsen, and Speaker Ed Jackamonis.

Employees at the General Motors plant in Janesville invited myself, Gov. Tony Earl (seated middle) and Senate Majority Leader Tim Cullen (at podium) to visit and answer questions.

I accompanied Gov. Tony Earl (center) on a campaign stop in DeForest. 10

Budget time again with (left to right) Majority Leader Dismas Becker; Michael Youngman, my administrative assistant; and Minority Leader Tommy Thompson. 11

12

Barbara and me with our sons, Alec (left) and Karl, in 1989 at the beginning of my last session in the Assembly.

Representative Government: What It Means in Theory and in Practice

It may well happen that the public voice, pronounced by the representatives of the people, will be more consonant to the public good than if pronounced by the people themselves.[1]

James Madison

Whoever wants to know the heart and mind of America had better learn baseball, the rules and realities of the game.[2]

Jacques Barzun

The United States has a representative system of government at the national level, in the U.S. House and U.S. Senate, and in the legislatures of the fifty states. But what does this mean? Americans have never agreed on the answer. John Adams, the second president, believed a representative legislature should be "an exact portrait, in miniature, of the people at large, as it should think, feel, reason and act like them." British statesman Edmund Burke, whose political philosophy influenced the founders, had a different view. "Your representative," wrote Burke, "owes you, not his industry alone, but his judgment, and he betrays, instead of serving you, if he sacrifices it to your opinion." The third president of the United States, Thomas Jefferson, emphasized the importance of democratic results:

---

[1] Alexander Hamilton, James Madison, and John Jay, *The Federalist Papers* (New York: New American Library, 1961), no. 10, 82.

[2] Jacques Barzun, *God's Country and Mine*, reprint of 1954 ed. (Westport, Conn.: Greenwood Press, 1973).

1

"governments are republican only in proportion as they embody the will of the people and execute it." [3]

I served in the Wisconsin legislature for fourteen years, the last eight as the Speaker of the Assembly. On many issues I think I embodied the will of the people, but sometimes—as several examples in this chapter explain—I did not think, feel, reason, and act like my constituents; I voted my conscience. This book is a personal account of my experience as a state representative from 1977 to 1991. The tales I tell, however, are not unique to my state. I discuss campaigns, political money, abortion politics, interest group politics, the legislative process, and ethics and lobbyists—issues relevant to every legislator in every state.

WISCONSIN: THE POLITICS OF FAIR PLAY

All legislators grapple with the challenge of being "representative," but each state has its own political culture. The moral, do-good culture of Wisconsin politics was stamped on the state like a brand by the "Progressives." First as the liberal faction of the Republican Party and then as a separate third party led by "Fighting Bob" LaFollette, the Progressives dominated political debate in the state from the turn of the century until the end of World War II.[4]

The Progressives believed in democracy, the educated citizen, and reform. They believed in the University of Wisconsin, where Bob LaFollette was graduated from in 1879. They believed that the university should exist to help common people and, most importantly, that it should be the problem-solving partner of state government. The Progressives took their best ideas from a brilliant cadre of social thinkers at the university. The result was the country's first progressive income tax, and national models for unemployment compensation, workers' compensation, and social security.

The Progressive Party disbanded in 1946 with the intention of once again becoming the dominant liberal wing of the Republican Party. However, a group of the younger Progressives (the "diaper brigade") rebelled at the idea that the GOP was their natural home. Instead they joined forces

---

[3] Fred R. Harris and Paul L. Hain, *America's Legislative Process: Congress and the States* (Glenview, Ill.: Scott, Foresman, and Co., 1983). The quote by Jefferson is on page 12, the quote by Adams is on page 13, and the quote by Burke is on page 18.

[4] "Fighting Bob" LaFollette was governor of Wisconsin from 1900 to 1906. He served in the U.S. Senate from 1906 until his death in 1925. The Progressive Party was then led by his sons—Robert Jr., who succeeded his father as U.S. senator and served until 1946, and Phil, who served as governor of Wisconsin for two terms in the 1930s.

with the small liberal wing of the Democratic Party, which was concentrated in Milwaukee, and with organized labor. Together they founded a new Democratic Party in Wisconsin. Thus, both the Republican and Democratic parties in the state have progressivism in their roots. This helps explain their activist, "government can help," character.

It is fair to state, as others have, that politics in Wisconsin (as in Minnesota, the Dakotas, and Iowa) has a moralistic streak. This particular brand of politics, which also can be called reform politics or citizen politics, dates back to the University of Wisconsin in LaFollette's day. LaFollette's mentor was Professor John Bascom. In his autobiography LaFollette describes Bascom as "the embodiment of moral force . . . feeling the new social forces . . . emphasizing the new social responsibilities . . . forever telling us what the state was doing for us and urging our return obligation not to use our education wholly for our own selfish benefit, but to return some service to the state." [5] This philosophy became the code of the Progressives.

The politics of fair play is evident in the state's unique open primary (another legacy from the Progressives). Each election Wisconsinites can choose to vote in either the Democratic or Republican primary. This reflects the Progressives' conviction that the people, not party bosses, should determine the candidates for political office.

As I stated earlier, each state has its political culture. Only a few examples are needed to give a flavor of the differences. Nebraska has a one-house legislature, and the candidates run without a party label. California voters, by collecting enough signatures on a petition, can place a proposal on a ballot. If a majority of those voting approve of the proposal, it becomes the law of the state; the legislature is bypassed. In Illinois the Chicago Democrats and the "downstate" Republicans meet, like the armies of two principalities, to do battle in the legislature. In some areas a dominant industry (for example, mining in Montana and aircraft in Seattle) explains the ways of politics and the legislature. In Massachusetts the Irish politicians of today fight for power with the scions of the Brahmins. This is the way it was, and this is the way it is. And it is probably safe to say that the old South fights for primacy with the new South almost every day in the legislatures of the former Confederacy.

Politically, states are different. The issues politicians face, however, are remarkably similar. In this way America's fifty state legislatures are more alike than different.

---

[5] *LaFollette's Autobiography* (Madison: University of Wisconsin Press, 1961).

THE MAKING OF A REPRESENTATIVE

When elected to a legislature, people start a new history, but they arrive fully formed. Politicians are not contemporary people. Representative government is more representative of the past—especially the representative's past—than the present.

For example, I always voted against changing the state's constitution to allow a state lottery because I arrived in the legislature believing that promoting gambling was not a legitimate function of government. If the people wanted this, then they were wrong.

I was brought up a Lutheran, a liberal brand, and was the grandson of Norwegian immigrants who came to Dane County, Wisconsin, to farm. These immigrants and their descendants became die-hard supporters of the agrarian populism of LaFollette and the Progressive movement. The paper my family read was the *Capital Times,* the Madison daily paper that was founded to support LaFollette and later fought Sen. Joe McCarthy. Even though 60 percent of my constituents favored a state lottery, I would not. Democrats of my stripe weren't for regressive taxes. Better that every Lutheran, Progressive, Norwegian, Dane County, *Capital Times* bone in my body crumble to dust than I vote for a lottery.

However, when the people of the state voted to change the constitution to allow a lottery, I felt obligated to vote for a bill that would implement the change. Why? Why, if I felt so strongly against a lottery did I feel after the referendum obligated to work for its implementation? Quite simply, the feeling of being a hired man came over me, and I believed it was my duty to carry out this directive. The debate was over and I lost.

My position also differed from most of my constituents on the mandatory seat belt law. I was quite bullheaded in my opposition to it because I objected to the federal government trying to force states to pass such bills or lose highway aid. Then my young son Alec changed my mind. Since infancy, he had always been buckled in, and one day he told his grandpa Adolph, who had never worn a seat belt, to click his belt so the car could start to move. This is what we always told him, and he now was telling his grandpa. What are you going to say? This is good for you, but grandpa has special protection from accidents? After Alec's comment, my position no longer depended on whether the federal government violated the spirit of federalism by withholding highway aid from states that did not pass the law (or on whether the mandatory law was a plot to exempt the auto companies from installing air bags).

My initial opposition to the mandatory seat belt law and my change of heart did not take into account the views of my constituents. Yet I felt any one of them, if asked to vote, might have done the same. Thus, I was representative of them.

Another example from my legislative career illustrates how representation is affected by a legislator's age and times. My grandparents' generation was shaped by immigration and World War I. My parents' generation was changed by the Great Depression and World War II. My generation came of age in the 1960s. Its views were influenced by the atomic bomb, civil rights, assassinations, the environmental movement, and the Vietnam War. The events that shape a generation are part of the making of a representative.

I voted twice against raising the drinking age (from eighteen to nineteen and later from nineteen to twenty-one). Only a few short years before the legislature had voted to lower the voting age and the drinking age, believing that if young men were old enough to fight and die in Vietnam, they were old enough to vote and drink. Had everyone forgotten this? I opposed both bills because to me it was the Vietnam War all over again. I would see my friend Freddie Suchomel's face, his fluid pitching motion, his name low on the wall of the Vietnam memorial on a clear winter day, so cold that even angry tears froze. I didn't care that 80 percent of my constituents were in favor of raising the drinking age, but I cared a lot that I not falter and commit an act of betrayal to my generation and vote yes.

A NEW BREED OF LEGISLATOR?

There has been talk by political scientists, pundits, and editorial writers about whether state legislatures are "representative" anymore. Some claim the young state legislator on the make, looking for a political career, has replaced the citizen legislator of the past. A Congressional Quarterly reporter once described me as part of this new breed of professional lawmakers: "Loftus is a full-time legislator—he has done nothing but political work since he left the University of Wisconsin." [6] An editorial in the *Milwaukee Journal* bemoaned the worldly inexperience of these politicians:

> Most troubling, the combination of youth and full-time political zeal usually means a lack of solid life experience beyond the campus and the capitol. Wisconsin voters increasingly are sending bright, young smart-alecks to Madison. You can tell them by their glib certitude—but you can't tell them much![7]

That statement is certainly one of parental exasperation. Nevertheless, the *Journal* almost always endorsed the smart alecks. It let me off the

---

[6] Alan Ehrenhalt, "Power Shifts in State Capitols As Professional Lawmakers Take Over Leadership Spots," *Congressional Quarterly Weekly Report,* September 3, 1983, 1767.

[7] *Milwaukee Journal,* September 18, 1983.

hook by saying that I had done much to "overcome" the new breed "handicap" and that I was an asset to the state.

In the 1980s and 1990s all kinds of political and societal happenings have mistakenly been attributed to the new "professional" lawmaker: the increase in interest groups, the rising costs of campaigns, increased spending by states, the need for term limits, and so on. When I was in elementary school, schoolchildren blamed inexplicable happenings on the Russians or on sun spots. To explain things by saying legislators today are somehow different than they used to be is in the sun spot category. Changes in state legislators from the imagined idyllic past can largely be explained by three things: reapportionment (which, among other things, brought minorities to the state legislatures); the election of more women to office (4 percent of state legislators in 1969, 20.4 percent in 1993); and the surrender to the states of many national responsibilities by the federal government. Other changes are primarily generational.

ARGUING FOR THE INEXPERIENCED

Tip O'Neill, the former Speaker of the U.S. House of Representatives, once said, "All politics is local." I would concur with the Speaker but add that politics is also generational. A generation is shaped in its youth. Wanting older politicians with "life experiences" is like saying Hemingway shouldn't have been published until he knew more. A legislature should have a critical mass of the young and inexperienced in life. Why? Because they are the most likely to believe they can get something done. Old people vote for young people to make things better. The young are not overly disheartened by the failures of others who have tried before them. Life can look long looking back or looking forward. Legislatures need to be weighted with those with the latter view.

Alexis De Tocqueville was a French politician, traveler, and historian who wrote extensively about nineteenth-century democracy in America. He once observed that in this country there were so many "ambitious men and so little lofty ambition." In his view the long bureaucratic apprenticeship required before gaining power creates an atmosphere where "lofty ambition breathes with difficulty." He goes on:

> All are indiscriminately subjected to a multitude of petty preliminary exercises, in which their youth is wasted and their imagination quenched, so that they despair of ever fully attaining what is held out to them; and when at length they are in a condition to perform any extraordinary acts, the taste for such things has forsaken them.[8]

---

[8] Alexis De Tocqueville, *Democracy in America*, specially edited and abridged for the modern reader by Richard D. Heffner (New York: Mentor, 1956), 259.

MORE CONTINUITY THAN CHANGE

State legislators today are like those that preceded them. They "are generally of higher social status than their constituents, especially in terms of education and occupational achievement. Few earn their living with their hands in what we usually call 'blue collar' occupations. Most are members of their district's dominant ethnic and religious groups." [9]

After all I did not arrive in Sun Prairie, Wisconsin, from Persia, a follower of Zoroaster, intending to sell band instruments to the high school and then end up somehow getting elected to the legislature. No, I represented the district where I was born. Like many of those I represented, I was raised a Lutheran and married a Catholic, can eat lutefisk with a smile, speak some Norwegian and some German, know how to play euchre, and, with the help of beer, can dance the polka. Like most of those I represented, I understand everything Garrison Keillor has to say.

When I started to campaign among the farmers of Dane County, I was not the first Loftus to come by. They knew my dad who sold farm machinery in the same area. Never once did a farmer I asked for a vote say he had been beat on a deal by him. They knew my cousin who sold crop insurance and my cousin who ran the lumber yard. They knew a lot about me and my politics and outlook on things, even though they may have been meeting me for the first time. They did not have to ask what kind of Democrat I was because the soil in Dane County usually produced only one kind. And they didn't think much about my occupation (a former speech writer and legislative aide), except when I advertised the fact, in order to get votes, that I was not a lawyer.

Today's legislators, whether considered "representative" or not, have occupations similar to their predecessors in political office. Lawyers and insurance and real estate types are still well represented. There are a lot fewer farmers because there are a lot fewer farms, and today there are some whose sole occupation is being a legislator. But you never could have a nine-to-five job in a factory or an office and expect to get elected. These types were not in legislatures before, and they aren't in them now.

Today there are a much greater number of flexible occupations: teachers, preachers, community activists and organizers, and those who because they are young and single, can just quit whatever they are doing and campaign all day for months. But it's still the same type of people attracted to politics.

---

[9] Fred Harris and Paul L. Hain, *America's Legislative Process: Congress and the States* (Glenview, Ill.: Scott, Foresman and Co., 1983).

Politics is challenge and risk, reward and satisfaction, and in most state legislatures, unlike the Congress, there is no apprenticeship, or waiting for the old boys to retire or the boss to keel over before one gets to make decisions and be in charge. Your productive years start when you arrive, regardless of your age.

Experienced or youthful, most people who hold elective office are there for the right reasons. They are there because voters chose them rather than their opponents. They fail because they are mortals who can succumb to temptation but not because they are unrepresentative.

A LEGISLATURE AS A BASEBALL TEAM

A legislature is like a baseball team (national league, no designated hitter). Each season the job is about the same. There are some rookies and some veterans, some stars and some utility players. A manager and coaches make hundreds of decisions on strategy every day in an effort to win, but mostly they are not in control of the outcome of the game. The rules remain the same each season, and there is an off-season when trades are made.

The teams are different in different states. Some teams have a history of spitters and bean balls; some teams have a history of fair play. It depends on the culture of the state.

The players all vary in talent and play different positions, but they have one thing in common—they are all in the big leagues. The manager works with what he's got. It is his job to win if possible, and if not, to be gracious about losing. Sometimes the fans are enthusiastic and loyal, sometimes they are sullen and want change. There is not much mystery to the game once you know the rules.

The Campaign:
Winning Votes One by One

The Americans determined that the members of the legislature should be elected by the people directly, and for a brief term, in order to subject them, not only to the general convictions but to the daily passions of their constituents.[1]

Alexis De Tocqueville

Most successful candidates for the legislature can do two things well: ask strangers for their vote and ask relatives and friends for money. Campaigning for the state legislature is a fairly intimate pursuit. In a hotly contested race, or a race without an incumbent, someone in a voter's household will probably meet one or both of the candidates during the course of a campaign.

In my first race for the Assembly in 1976,[2] I started my day with the goal of shaking hands with eighty people before 2:00 P.M. On easy days I found a line somewhere to accomplish this task; lunch time at a senior citizens' center was the best target of opportunity. Then I went door to door, working up and down streets with a list of the names and addresses of the regular voters. About 5:00 P.M. , after my wife Barbara left work, we would knock on doors together until dark, about 8:30 or 9:00 in the summer.

On Friday nights in September and October, we attended high school football games in the district. At the gate where the home team fans en-

---

[1] Alexis De Tocqueville, *Democracy in America*, specially edited and abridged for the modern reader by Richard D. Heffner (New York: Mentor, 1956), 112.

[2] The Assembly is one of the houses in Wisconsin's bicameral legislature. The other is the Senate.

tered, we shook hands and handed out a small card printed with that high school's season on one side and the Green Bay Packers' schedule on the reverse. We rejoiced when it got cold enough so we could see our breath, and we would turn and exhale puffs of October at each other because this meant that the November election was near.

Every Saturday morning I would be shaking hands outside a grocery store in one town, while Barbara was staked out in a similar place in another town. On weekend afternoons we directed crews of volunteers in a systematic distribution of literature throughout the district. Volunteers would come to our house in the morning for donuts and coffee, get their map and their packs of literature, and be off. And then we would go, too. More friends, and friends of friends, came on Saturday. Sundays found the two of us stuffing literature in the doors on the blocks that were not finished.

In the last weeks I greeted morning shifts at plant gates. Every election day I pumped hands outside the porcelain factory in Sun Prairie. It was partly superstition. In my first campaign the owners of this factory, a family from my home town, had invited my Republican opponent to go inside, and in this and other ways let it be known that I was not their choice. However, when I appeared outside the plant gate, and waited there shivering in the cold early on election day, it became a blow against the bosses to vote for me. I never asked to go in that factory, and every election morning I was there shaking hands outside the gate, still presumably shut out.

EDUCATING THE CANDIDATE

Some think campaigns are to educate the voters. They are wrong. The purpose, from the candidate's perspective, is to win. However, the actual outcome of a campaign is to educate the candidate about his or her district. All the handshaking, all the pleasantries exchanged, help make a politician representative. If you talk to people at their doors, on the threshold of their homes, and glimpse their families and perhaps their furniture and the pictures on the walls, you will begin to see their dreams realized and not realized, and you will begin to understand your prospective constituents.

The first thing you will know is that there is a big barking dog behind every third door who has not read the *Federalist Papers* or from the looks of the yard has much to do with papers at all. I soon learned to lodge my foot against the bottom of the door so the dog would not get out—a sure way to lose a vote. I also did this for protection; I was bitten twice.

At first I was surprised at how many people were home during the day. Such a revelation is part of the picture of the district that was painted in my mind. The ages, the poverty, the wealth, the cars, the bumper stickers on the cars, the NRA sticker on the pickup, the kids, the fishing boat, the piano, the antlers on the garage, the accents, the Christian fish decal by the doorbell, the garden, the tattoos—all of these things help form the candidates' view of the people they hope to represent.

Another indelible memory is of the many mothers at home with an adult child who is disabled or retarded. They are there in a neat living room, a picture of a soldier and a graduate on a table, and often a framed picture of John Kennedy on the wall. "Oh, won't you come in?" I was usually asked. I almost always turned down the invitation because my need was to move on to finish the list for that day. But sometimes I did enter the house. One elderly woman asked me to please come in because it was lunch time, and she was feeding her daughter, and she knew of my family. We talked about old people when they were young as she gently placed a spoon of soup to her daughter's lips. She had been taking care of her daughter for fifty years.

BONDING WITH THE VOTER

Most people are pleased when a candidate comes to their door. A candidate may not be as welcome as the UPS man, but neither is he or she an evangelist trying to convert you or a kid selling band pizza. Many political scientists underestimate the importance of bonding between voter and candidate. Lyndon Johnson, as a member of Congress and as president, knew that people had to be touched. Think of how many times you have heard someone say when asked about a politician, "I shook his hand." They do not talk of issues or votes. They say, "I never met him," or "I went to school with his sister," or "I heard him speak. He is taller than on television."

Here is the pitch of a losing candidate at a voter's doorstep:

Hello, I am John Jones and I am running for the Assembly in the Forty-Sixth District. Do you have any questions?

Here is the patter of a winning candidate at the door:

Hello, my name is Tom Jones and I'm running for the Assembly, and I just stopped by to introduce myself. (Shake hands.) What is your name? Well, it is a pleasure to meet you Mrs. Smith. May I give you a piece of my campaign literature. (Hand it to her.) That's my family. The youngest is in kindergarten. It was a pleasure to meet you. Don't forget to vote. I hope to get your vote! Goodbye. Nice flowers.

The idea is to meet the voter, shake hands, banter a bit, *ask for a vote*, and leave. If you ask, "Are there any questions?" you risk making someone uncomfortable. People do not know, or think they know, exactly what office you are talking about, and often they don't know if there is an incumbent. They would be embarrassed if their question was not intelligent. Five minutes at a door is way too long. I did not visit farms, except to place a sign on a barn next to the road; there was not time. There were more than 13,000 houses and apartments in my district. My first race I hit every one and knocked on the doors of the targeted voters twice!

Usually I worked from a list of names and would say when the door was answered, "Hello, Mrs. Smith. I am. . . ." No one was taken aback. Most thought it a compliment that I somehow knew their name. People want to know that others know who they are. They want to know they are important. The list would also tell me how many voters were in the house, and whether they were A, B, or C voters. My list would be annotated by my sisters. They would note such things as whether I went to school with someone's daughter, or if the son was a basketball player, or if someone had just married or died.

DETERMINING A, B, C, AND D VOTERS

It is unlikely a candidate will win if he or she spends time at the doors talking to people who do not vote. A sin worse than actually talking to nonvoters, which for reasons of politeness often can't be avoided, is spending money to mail things to nonvoters. It may be someone's job or cause to moan about those who fail to vote, but it is not the candidate's. Elections are not decided by those who are too lazy or too turned off to vote. (As one sage nonvoter admitted, "I don't vote. It only encourages them.")

Commitments for votes are collected one at a time. It is piece work, and it is hard, like picking BB's off a driveway. A commitment must be verified. Thus, a list of voters is needed. The list of registered voters is obtained from the city or town clerk. A lot of the voters on these lists are dead or have moved because the list is cleansed only in five-year cycles. Many will vote only in presidential election years, and quite a few in this group will vote only for president, skipping races below this on the ballot, like those for the state legislature. In nonpresidential election years there is also a considerable drop-off in voting from the races at the top of the ticket—U.S. senator or governor—to those below. So the list of registered voters must be coded in a way to identify those who usually vote.

The A voter is the one who has voted in all the races the campaign has decided to use. Why not simply target those who voted in the most recent election? Although this universe may be big enough, it is not good enough because it is the consistent voter over time who must be the target of the candidate's affection and the campaign's money.

Assume the upcoming election, "your" election, is a September primary. The voter who voted only in the last general election becomes a D voter. The voter who has voted in this election plus one of the last three partisan primaries is a C voter. The B voter has voted in the last general election and two of the three primaries, and an A voter has voted in all four elections. The A list will be small, and these voters will be older.

This categorized list of voters is needed for several reasons: only a few of these voters will be dead; the campaign will waste less money if it has the discipline to concentrate its resources on these voters; and the candidate will actually talk to people who have voted in the past and are likely to vote in the future. The crux of the campaign for state legislature is to find likely voters and persuade a majority of them to vote for you. Some think elections to the state legislature are won or lost based on a candidate's stand on issues. In most cases they are wrong. The winning campaign is usually the one which, after finding the right pool of voters, identifies supporters and then drags them out to the polls.

During the course of the campaign, A, B, C, and D voters are further classified. A voter who tells the candidate at the door, "Yes, I will vote for you," or who responds positively to a telephone survey conducted by the campaign, becomes a 1 voter. A voter who otherwise somehow indicates that he or she will probably vote for the candidate becomes a 2 voter, called a "leaner" in secret insider talk. Voters who say they don't know how they will vote are a 3. Voters who say they are going to vote for the other candidate become a 4, and care is taken not to spend money on them or inadvertently remind them there is an election in the offing. The A, B, C, and D voters who are eventually identified as either 1, 2, or 3 become the focus of the campaign at the end. The goal is to make them all A1 voters.

PREDICTING THE VOTE

In a partisan race most who vote will vote the way they voted in the past. And it will likely be how their parents voted. Historical voting patterns in an area, whether for the state legislature or Congress, hold over time. In America party loyalty is weak until the person enters the voting booth. Partisan allegiance changes because of events, such as the Great Depression, or because of persuasive leaders, such as Franklin Delano Roosevelt and Ronald Reagan. Sometimes party allegiance changes as part of a general cyclical swing in the country toward conservatism or liberalism. In most state legislative districts, however, the percentage of the vote each party will get is quite predictable.

When an incumbent leaves office (an open seat race), predicting the vote becomes more difficult. Unless a district is extremely partisan, it is up for grabs. In this circumstance there are more than enough voters who can easily vote for the "right" person in either party.

Something like an "open seat" can occur when reapportionment moves an incumbent into new territory, or if a district experiences a population shift that changes the partisan complexion. For example, if urban Democrats move to the suburbs, they will continue their partisan habits, and a "safe" Republican incumbent soon would be in trouble.

The most important races for the state legislature fall into two categories: primaries in highly partisan districts with an open seat (because the winner of the primary in effect wins the seat) and general elections in districts where either party could reasonably expect to win (usually called marginal districts). The key races are the ones in these latter districts when there is an open seat.

THE VOTER'S DECISION

A decision to vote for one of the two candidates in an open seat for the state legislature is a serious decision that is not really rethought the next time around. The persuadable voter is wooed by two suitors and, having chosen one, does not two years later divorce and choose again between the incumbent and a new Romeo. Incumbents are hard to beat partly because of the bond they form with voters during their first campaign.

The next campaign, and others that will follow, will be a choice for voters between the known incumbent and the unknown challenger. Asking voters to vote against the incumbent is like asking them to discard an old friend in order to gain a new friend. Most of us would stick with the old friend. Isn't the logic of term limits, "Stop me, before I vote for him again!"?

The gentle Earl McEssy served in the Wisconsin legislature for over thirty years, and his slogan in his last few elections actually was, "Don't trade an old friend for a new friend." Earl was loved by all, including me, but eventually voters did trade him for a new friend. When I went to his district to endorse the Democratic challenger, I specifically mentioned the pension Earl could expect if he was defeated. Perhaps this made it a little easier for his friends to vote for his opponent.

LEARNING FROM A STATE CAMPAIGN

Working on Harland Everson's first reelection campaign for the Assembly in 1972 helped me solve the "mystery" of running for office. It was an important step for me, one that took me from wanting to run for the state legislature, to planning to run.

Harland represented the district next to Sun Prairie, the district where I lived. He was one of those Norwegian farmers who raised tobacco and chewed it, but he was not typical of them because he had a university degree and owned the weekly newspaper in his town. One day he stopped at my dad's business to buy a part for a tractor and, in the course of the conversation, mentioned he needed someone to help with his campaign. The message got to me, and I gave him a call, and the next thing I knew I was running the campaign. The assets were Harland's good name, and a small group of loyal volunteers. There was no pay (I admit I did fill the gas tank in my green Mustang at Harland's farm), but I was thrilled to do it. I was fresh out of graduate school and working as a house painter, and I was looking for a job in politics.

As I said, the successful candidate can ask a stranger for a vote and ask a friend for money. Harland could do neither. He went to every meeting in his district, his year-round method of campaigning, but listening is what he did best. He was not good at small talk, and he was no orator. Once at a supper for candidates endorsed by the teachers' union, Harland was asked to say a few words. He stood up, walked to the front, and faced the group. He tried to talk but could not. He tried again, and this went on for an agonizing time. Finally, I started to applaud and the others joined in and Harland smiled sheepishly and sat down. He had thought the words would come, and usually they did. No one was embarrassed, or talked of this to others because they knew of his goodness and the works in his life. It wasn't what he did in life; it was how he had gone about doing it that was known and admired.

That campaign I roamed through eastern Dane County, the same territory where my dad sold farm machinery. I tacked campaign signs on barns and placed them in store windows on the main streets; I delivered ads to the seven weekly newspapers; and I organized mailings. Voter lists weren't even thought about nor were bulk mailing permits. Harland would print up thousands of campaign fliers at the newspaper shop and then take a load to his house in his truck. I would stuff my small car full of the heavy bundles till the tires nearly touched the fender wells, drive to my mother's house, and lug my cargo to her large blonde oak dining room table. In the graceful Palmer Method handwriting they had been taught in grade school, my mother and her sister (my Aunt Mildred) would address a flier to everyone listed in the phone book. Then the task changed to licking stamps (first-class stamps paid for, like everything else, out of Harland's pocket). My sisters Shirley and Jerry helped, and Jerry organized the resulting piles for mailing. I was good on stamps, having perfected the damp wash cloth method of wetting the glue. Preparing the mailings was fun for all. There was coffee, and my father would bring sweet rolls for the workers.

Years later when we were both members of the Assembly, Harland and I were placed in the same district after a federal judge reapportioned the districts. Harland decided to retire. He said I was too young to quit, and it would be wrong to run against each other. When he passed away, his family asked me to speak at his funeral service in the Lutheran Church in Edgerton, and this was a great honor for me.

LEARNiNG FROM A PRESIDENTIAL CAMPAIGN

I learned some things about organization and a lot about people by managing Harland's campaign, but it was the Udall for President campaign where I learned about real organization and the A, B, C, 1, 2, 3 voters. It was also where I met a great human being.

Rep. Morris Udall from Arizona, everyone called him Mo, had a great sense of humor and was once a professional basketball player. He often said, "We need a president who can stuff it." At the time of this race, I was working for the Speaker of the Assembly; he supported Udall because he was known as an environmentalist. I supported Udall because the Speaker did and because after Vietnam, Watergate, and Nixon's pardon, I felt, like most Democrats, that 1976 must be our year.

The organizing started almost two years prior to the 1976 primary election, which is held the first Tuesday in April in Wisconsin. At the first organizing meeting of the Udall followers, I was volunteered to be the Dane County chair by a friend who worked in the majority leader's office. This wasn't planned, but when it happened everyone was relieved, like kids in class who knew they would not now be called on.

Because Dane County is a gold mine of votes in a Democratic primary, and events would dictate that Mo's strategy would be to meet and beat Jimmy Carter in Wisconsin, it was an intense campaign. I devoted every spare moment to the effort. There was no pay (and no free gas). In fact, I had to lend my car to the campaign.

By the time of the election, such things as registration lists, phone banks, voter ID, and targeting had lost their mystery. I had become, through trial and error (there was a lot of room for error) quite adept at "advancing" a visit—building a crowd, framing an event as a picture for the TV news, and briefing reporters. I had met and become friends with hundreds of volunteers working on a campaign that they loved working on because of the civility and humor and loyalty of the candidate.

We almost won. The TV networks called Mo the winner late election night, and I went to bed rejoicing. But as that night wore on, the paper ballots in the rural areas were counted and Carter won by a handful. Mo later wrote a book entitled *Too Funny to be President*. Perhaps he did lose because he displayed his humor or wrongly thought wit the better part of political discourse. But he left the country, and the many he met, including me, better for trying.

Ten years later I visited him in his office in the House, where he was the Interior Committee chairman. He had Parkinson's disease, and his head would bob because of the condition. He autographed a copy of his book, and we talked of the great presidential primary in Wisconsin in April 1976.

Less than one month after that primary, I quit my job as the administrative assistant to the Speaker, announced my candidacy for the legislature, and started to campaign full time. The seat was open, something I had known for two years because the incumbent, David O'Malley, had told me he was retiring.

Reapportionment had given the district some new territory, including my home town of Sun Prairie. This new turf, plus the fact that David had been many years in the political wars and had started to look frail, had prompted a challenge from a young, aggressive Republican with strong ties to the area. David had won reelection by a slim margin, and the same opponent had let it be known that she would run against him again. A Democrat from his toes to his nose, David did not want "his" district to "go Republican," and he knew this meant he had to bow out. God rest his good Irish soul, he tipped me off to his plans.

Like most of the people I would serve with in the legislature, I was self-recruited. I had moved back to Sun Prairie in anticipation of running for David O'Malley's seat in the Assembly, even before I knew of his retirement plans. By the time I quit my job, I had the plan for the campaign in my head.

MY FIRST PRIMARY CAMPAIGN

Voter registration is required in most places in this country, and in many states voters also must declare their party identification. A voter registers as a Democrat, a Republican, or an Independent. Thus, a Democratic candidate (in Illinois, New York, California, and many other states) works from a list of registered voters who have already indicated that they plan to vote in the Democratic primary. This is not the case, however, in Wis-

consin. The Progressives believed in the open primary that allows qualified voters to choose the party primary of their choice at any given primary election. Wisconsin is also unique because voter registration is
required by state law only in communities of more than 5,000. Consequently, in my race there were lists of registered voters available only in
Sun Prairie and Middleton, the two small cities in the district.

TARGETING VOTERS

These two lists were acquired easy enough, but they noted only the
registered voters, not the elections they had previously voted in. To make
up a new list of targeted voters, I had to borrow the old lists from the four
elections we had selected in order to check off who actually voted.

My sister Shirley sat at her kitchen table day after day that spring
making a master list. She lives at the end of a cul-de-sac, and every morning I would drive down MacArthur Street to pick up a door-to-door list. I
knew she would be there, and this was important to me. Being a candidate
is a lonely affair. Like a pilot, you must know there are those back at the
field who helped you leave and care that you return.

For the areas without lists I borrowed the books for each village and
town for each of the four targeted elections, and a new list was made from
whole cloth. The only thing in these "books," actually lined tablets with
manila covers, was the names of the voters and their addresses. Since this
information was in the clerk's handwriting, and each clerk had a different
system, it took forever and assumed a lot of local knowledge. For example,
"Shorty Olson" would be followed by "Mrs. Shorty Olson," and the address would be Route 1. My mother and my sisters would match the
names with the telephone book and call a friend in the area to find out
who was married to whom. In this way we could get all the voters at one
address together and find out which Olson was called "Shorty."

CONTACTING VOTERS

To place a candidate's name on the ballot, residents of the district
must sign a nomination paper. Only 200 signatures are required for an
Assembly race in Wisconsin. On the first day that nomination papers
could be circulated, a cool sunny day in late spring, I took Shirley's new
list of A voters in the second ward in Sun Prairie and knocked at these
doors, and only these doors, to ask for a signature. I continued to go to the
doors of A voters until the deadline for circulating papers had passed.

I was asking only for their signature in order that my name could be
on the ballot. It was too early to ask for a vote, but it was a contact with a
sure voter. I worked hard, sometimes talking like a salesman laying the

groundwork for a future sale, sometimes chatting like a bashful boyfriend, poised to leave but not leaving, lingering for a kiss.

The next day the volunteer crew, which had grown to include my mother-in-law, Bernice Schasse, and my former Sunday School teacher, Jeanette Renk, mailed all the A voters I had visited the day before a postcard thanking them for their hospitality. (This process would be repeated later as I moved through the B, C, and D voters.) In addition to mailing postcards, the kitchen table platoon busily transcribed Shirley's list onto three-by-five cards, where they noted the names of all the voters at one address; whether they were A, B, C, or D voters; and the telephone number. Later the 1, 2, 3 notation would be added to these cards.

Closer to the primary election, after I had been to several thousand doors and had more knowledge of the campaign, the invaluable card file was distributed to another set of friends and volunteers. From their homes they would call, and after a couple of preliminary questions to break the ice (for example, confirming the address), the voter would be asked, "If the election were held tomorrow, would you vote for Tom Loftus?" Depending on the reply, the volunteer would mark the card 1, 2, or 3. All the cards would then be returned to campaign headquarters to be sorted for the get-out-the-vote telephone campaign on election day.

Another part of the primary campaign involved targeted mailings. The list was prepared from Shirley's work. For example, the A and B voters in rural areas would receive a letter signed by a list of farmers supporting me. If the campaign had an event, like a fund raiser, a list of local sponsors would be printed on the invitation, and it would be sent to all the A and B voters. They would surely see a friend or neighbor on the list of those supporting me and probably think that is why they were invited.

The whole process of contacting voters in Sun Prairie was duplicated by another team in Middleton, thirty miles away on the West side of the district. This team was headed by Verna Hill, Nan Cheney, and Pat Levin; all three were campaign veterans who had worked with me on the Udall campaign and knew what it took to get a vote. By election day three hundred volunteers had done something in the campaign, and on election day, the only day that counts, most of them had a specific task.

THE DAY OF THE PRIMARY

My campaign headquarters, the former showroom of the Dodge and Chrysler dealership in Sun Prairie, was the J&L Garage. Two auto mechanics (John and Larry) changed oil and ground valves and rented me an unused part of the building for $50 a month. The background noise heard on the headquarter's one phone was the machine gun staccato of John's air wrench trying to break a lug nut free from 35,000 miles of rust.

At the time, 1976, most campaigns for the state legislature went without the luxury of a campaign headquarters, but I needed a place to go other than my mother's house. I also needed a place where the camaraderie of a successful campaign could incubate. Headquarters is where the campaign of election day started.

The night before, my volunteer "poll watchers" had stopped by to receive the stack of index cards for their ward and written instructions explaining that they did indeed have the right to sit next to the poll worker and see the names of those who voted. When a Loftus supporter voted, the poll watcher removed that card from the stack. In this way we kept track of which of our supporters (the 1s and 2s) had voted, so we could concentrate on hunting down the remainder.

At 4:00 P.M. the poll watchers quit and returned their cards to headquarters. The cards of those supporters who had not yet voted were separated, stacked into packs of fifty, and secured with a rubber band. Between 4:30 and 5:00 these cards were picked up by other volunteers who quickly returned to their homes to start to phone. (Shirley took two stacks.) This effort was organized by my Aunt Eileen. The former Chrysler dealership hadn't seen this much traffic since the day the '59 Imperial arrived in town and everyone turned out to look at its two-foot-high fins and dual headlights that looked like chrome eyeballs floating between the bumper and the hood.

The phoners called our supporters and asked them to please vote. What is more, the phoners were instructed to ask them what time they thought they would vote. After that time passed, the phoners called back to make sure our identified voters actually had voted. Volunteers in Middleton duplicated this operation with the supporters on their lists. In the rural areas and the small towns there were no poll watchers, so the phoning started earlier in the day.

I won the primary with a total of 2,669 votes. As I said election night, "It was all organization." There were about 2,400 1s and 2s in our card file. Lawyer Tom Hebl, a high school friend and college roommate, came in second (1,472 votes); Richard Keller, a dairy farmer, came in third (865 votes); and Jim Bailey, a lawyer, came in fourth (565 votes). Friends before the race, the three of us became better friends after the election. They have been loyal supporters of me through my whole political life.

THE GENERAL ELECTION

The primary turnout of 5,571 voters on the Democratic side was quite high because it was a spirited race for an open seat. The winning candidate had a chance to win in the general election and would likely hold the seat for a number of years. There should be no mystery about this notion. When they cast their ballots in an open seat contest, voters know they are probably choosing a representative for a long time. This choice starts with the primary voters in both parties.

In the general election campaign we repeated the tactics used in the primary election. However, because of the much bigger voter base, the campaign concentrated on mass mailings. All rural addresses, and all registered voters regardless of their voting history, were mailed a brochure that was general in nature rather than one targeted to a group or focused on one issue. I continued going door to door, and by November my face was as tan as a farmer's neck and my belly as flat as the day I finished basic training. A campaign is physical more than mental. Good legs beat good ideas most of the time.

When deciding who to vote for in a race for the state legislature, people are influenced by those who have met the candidate. That's why shaking hands door to door is so important. Personal contact with the candidate often causes voters to look a little closer at the brochures, the ads, and the newspaper stories, and to become part of a word-of-mouth campaign that is as real as the real campaign. It all boils down to coffee. To win a candidate must be talked about over coffee. It is this coffee talk, with its own rituals and manners, that can decide the outcome of the race.

> OLE: "Who you voting for for Assembly?"
> LARS: "It won't be Jones unless he is better than his old man at paying bills on time. I might vote for Smith because he's young. We need to get some of those old ones like us out of there."
> OLE: "I see Jones is endorsed by the *Journal*."
> LARS: "That's a Republican paper. Hell, they endorsed Joe McCarthy. That's a good reason not to vote for Jones."
> OLE: "Have you met Smith?"
> LARS: "He come to my door. That's his cousin who runs the bakery, you know. They have his sign in the window. Who you voting for?"
> OLE: "I was thinking of Smith."
> LARS: "Who do the Cubs play today?"

I won the general election in 1976 because of the sound organizational work in the primary and because of the high turnout for the presidential election. Jimmy Carter did well in my area. It was also a good year for Democrats because the memory of Watergate still haunted the GOP. The vote was Loftus, 13,293; Republican Shirley Thompson, 10,446; Independent Edith Schreiber, 89—a sizable turnout in a district whose boundaries corralled fewer than 50,000 people.

My winning percentage of the vote (56 percent) was more or less what past voting history indicated a Democrat could expect in the Sun Prairie district. I won the same predictable percentage of the vote in every election in which I had a credible and hard-working Republican opponent with some money. It didn't matter whether it was a presidential election year or not. After incumbency had set in, and I no longer had serious challengers, my winning percentage went up. (Incumbency sets in when people think that anyone would be foolish to run against the incumbent, and even partisans on the other side start to say, "He can't be beat.")

It is not enough to have a predictable percentage of the population behind you. You have to believe in yourself and in your ability to win. The real advantage incumbents have is that they have won before. They know the twists and turns of the track, and they know they must be ahead of their opponent only on the last stretch of the last lap. That old campaign manager Aesop said it best: "slow and steady wins the race."

PRESS COVERAGE

A race for the state legislature usually receives only cursory press attention. There is a story when the candidates announce. There is a "profile" of the race. There is usually an endorsement by a newspaper, and the results are reported the morning after the election. If the TV market is small, there will be a story or two, visual versions of the same ilk as the newspaper stories. In bigger markets, candidates for the state legislature can expect to see themselves on the TV news only on election night, and then only if they won and the race was close.

There was a little more coverage of the race between Shirley Thompson and me because it was an open seat contest. A weekly paper in each town in the district would usually run our press releases. In the two daily papers in Madison, however, we had little more than the profile, the endorsement, and the results. We both bought some radio and a little TV. Mine was a thirty-second spot—a series of still pictures with a voice over. It played for the five days before the election on the noon news show on the local CBS affiliate.

Both in the primary and the general election campaigns, there were some debates, but their impact was limited for the most part to those actually in the audience. These are polite affairs before the Rotary Club or some other group willing to eat soft food at lunch. The two candidates make statements, and then the audience asks them questions. Unless a candidate for the state legislature suggests that the state secede or reveals that he or she once was held captive in a flying saucer, little note will be taken of anything said during a debate, but it is another part of the coffee talk campaign.

A LONGTIME INCUMBENT

I never met my opponent in my last reelection campaign. Once from my car window I spotted him on the street distributing literature, but that was it. "How can this be?" you ask. Well, a longtime incumbent in what is considered to be a safe seat enjoys different rules.

First, people with some base in the community and some ability to raise money do not run for office because they assume there is little chance of winning. These types wait for a fighting chance, and usually this chance occurs only when the seat opens up or reapportionment changes the voter mix. Furthermore, the political parties or party committees in the legislature focus resources on the marginal seats (seats obtained in the last election by a slim majority). Candidates who oppose a popular incumbent are not even led to believe they will get outside help.

Second, the press is horse-race driven. In other words, unless there is a likelihood of a close contest and a possible upset, the press will pay no attention to the race, let alone to the challenger. The intern from the journalism school will be relieved from writing obituaries on a slow death day and assigned the one story this race will be allotted. And the story will be worse for the challenger than no news at all.

> He's given almost no chance of winning against popular vote-getter Representative Smith, and has little money, but Candidate Jones thinks voters are fed up and is predicting a surprise for his lonely campaign this coming Tuesday. . . .

Third, voters do not approach each election thinking their past judgments about the incumbent were mistakes. The seven times I was elected to the legislature, I had three credible Republican opponents and one solo crusader with an interesting past who ran as a Republican; he made it somewhat of a race because he concentrated on the issue of crime. (His "stop crime" signs, replicas of highway stop signs, were everywhere, and I almost fainted when he won the straw vote among the students at Stoughton High School.) I would contend in three more elections, but my opponents were paid scant attention. They were challengers who simply could not be considered serious.

Voters are not going to take a look at a candidate who is given no chance of winning. I never met my opponent in my final campaign for the legislature because not one Rotary Club, Kiwanis Club, American Legion, Chamber of Commerce, labor union, or other group ever invited the two of us to speak. I felt bad that I did not meet this fellow, but my life was consumed with raising money and campaigning in other parts of the state for Democrats in marginal seats. The Democrats would remain in the majority, and I would continue to be the Speaker, only if they won. My last campaign in my district was short and simple: my family and the core group of volunteers from the first campaign distributed one piece of literature, a recycled update from the previous campaign, on the last two weekends before the election. I never hit a door.

WHO WINS AND WHY

There are important issues in a race for the state legislature, but they do not determine the outcome. In my first campaign the only issue that could sway a few voters was my stand in favor of giving public school teachers the right to bargain collectively. In most campaigns the real issue is the comfort level the voter has with the candidate.

For the voter a campaign is a process of learning what to expect, as far as voting and conduct, from each candidate if he or she is elected. A campaign is two salespeople selling a similar product at the same price. The winner is not necessarily the one with the best pitch but the one the voter feels most comfortable with. This factor is intangible, and it comes into play only with those voters who will switch parties, and usually only when there is an open seat or when a longtime incumbent is unexpectedly retired for no apparent reason. The challenger also has a dark suit and can tie a tie and seems nice enough—a pretty typical Republican or Democrat. So the voters decide they need a change and, what the heck, at the last minute they switch allegiance and trade in their Chevy for a Ford.

The only thing voters know for certain about a candidate running for the state legislature is whether that person is a Republican or a Democrat. Then the question is: what kind of Republican or Democrat? After these clues to comfort and predictability are discovered, the next step is to make some judgment about character and the type of person right for the times. At this point the candidate's age, family, experience, occupation, and education become factors.

Shirley Thompson was a moderate Republican, active in community affairs, and she had almost won the district against a longtime incumbent the election before we met. We both had family throughout the district, and we both ran good campaigns. I probably won because the district was slightly Democratic, and I was right for the times, and this tipped it between seeming equals.

My campaign slogan was "A New Face You'll See Again." The first comment by the conservative editor of my hometown paper was, "It's good to see two of our youthful members of the community running for the state Assembly. . . . They bring youth and enthusiasm to the office." After the primary the liberal *Capital Times* noted, "Loftus epitomizes the young new thrust of the party." Youth was in the year I ran. The retiring incumbent was sixty-four years old and from another era when the holder of the municipal office eventually moved up to the state legislature. Those times were gone, and change was the order of the day.

CAMPAIGNING THEN AND NOW

There have been few basic changes in campaigns for the state legislature in the past twenty years. Campaigns have become more high tech, but the basic task remains the same: finding likely supporters and making sure they go to the polls on election day and cast their ballot for you. Computers have reduced some of the handwork involved but not much. What my sister Shirley did with a pencil and a typewriter is now "entered" by someone sitting at a computer keyboard. Today the list of A, B, and C voters is easier to manipulate, but the process is the same: finding your voter one at a time. The real change has been in money—the amount, where it comes from, where it goes. I discuss these changes in financing elections in the next chapter.

Political Money: Reforms and Results

Money is the mother's milk of politics.[1]

Jess Unruh

It is impossible to get elected without campaign money. The pursuit of this money, however, can suck the moral core out of a politician. Jess Unruh, the Speaker of the California Assembly from 1961 to 1969, invented the current system of funneling big money through party leaders of state legislatures for distribution to candidates in marginal seats. His mother's milk remark is a concise way to say that "money is an important part of our political process, so stop worrying about it."

The politician who can get the money and get elected but not lose his or her soul in the process is the norm. However, the higher the politician climbs toward real power, the more likely the pursuit of political money will claim the talent and the purpose that have powered the ascent. Ted Sorenson, who was President John F. Kennedy's speech writer, recently put it this way in a speech of his own: "Clearly, power corrupts. Even worse, corruption is built into the very path to power for our national elected officials." Although he affirmed his belief that public life in America could be a "proud and lively career," Sorenson bemoaned a system that had become a chase after cash to finance the retention of power without purpose.[2]

---

[1] Quoted in Alan Rosenthal, *Legislative Life* (New York: Harper & Row, 1981), 118.
[2] This speech was delivered October 25, 1991, at the Institute of Politics, John F. Kennedy School of Government, Harvard University. The occasion was a dinner celebrating the twenty-fifth anniversary of the Institute.

A DANGEROUS PURSUIT

One example is as good as a thousand examples to demonstrate this. Consider one little scene from the savings and loan scandal that involved, among many, Alan Cranston, a distinguished U.S. senator from California who was a serious contender in 1984 for the Democratic nomination for president. The Senate Ethics Committee investigated whether five senators, including Cranston and former astronaut hero John Glenn, used their office to illegally help Charles Keating, a major contributor to the five. In particular, the committee investigated whether the senators pressured regulators to overlook the cooked books of an Arizona savings and loan run by Keating. Cranston stated that he needed huge amounts of money to run for reelection in his large state and, in a rather matter of fact way, revealed that this required him to spend five or six or sometimes seven hours a day on the telephone asking for money.

Cranston defended this daily dialing for dollars by saying the system made him do it. Most people, I would venture to guess, probably had a different view. A seventy-two-year-old senator in the twilight of an exemplary career who spends seven hours of any day begging for money so he can serve another six years is not a victim. He is a person who has become flawed, not the victim of a flawed system.

It is best to think of money in politics not as mother's milk or as poison but as water. If you have too little water, you die of thirst. If you have too much water, you drown. An inch of water is enough to slake thirst, and it is also enough to drown in if you are prostrate with your face down in it.

FINANCING MY FIRST CAMPAIGN

I can still recite almost all of the names of the people who contributed money to my first campaign for the Assembly in 1976. Lew Brooks, my father's partner, gave me $100, which was the largest single contribution, excluding that from my father or mother. A check for $25 was something of note and would produce a gasp of awe when mentioned to volunteers. The county Democratic party gave me $800, and the state party gave me $500. The AFL-CIO and the United Auto Workers contributed $400 each. The teachers' union gave $300, and the firefighters' union chipped in $100.

A little over $11,000 was spent in my first campaign, and that includes both the primary and the general election. This was the most money spent in an Assembly race in Wisconsin that year (1976). In the mid-1990s this amount would still buy a decent campaign for the Assembly, but the norm for an open seat or a marginal seat is around $50,000.

The money I raised in my first campaign came from relatives, friends, and Democrats in Dane County who were regular contributors to candidates for the state legislature. This was partisan money. The money from the party and the unions traditionally allied with the Democratic Party was also partisan money. In other words, most of my money came from people or groups who wanted to see a Democrat elected rather than a Republican. They had no immediate specific agenda or special interest (although the teachers were fighting for a bill to give them the right to bargain collectively), but they knew from history that their general interests would be better served by electing a Democrat. My Republican opponent, Shirley Thompson, raised her money in almost exactly the same way. It was also money from relatives and friends and partisan money from individuals and groups traditionally allied with the Republican Party—doctors, utilities, the Farm Bureau. They knew from history that their general interests would be better served by electing a Republican.

The chiropractors supported me with money because I supported a bill that would mandate that health insurance plans pay for chiropractic care. If Shirley Thompson had supported their position on this one bill, and I had been noncommittal, they would have given her money rather than me. Their special interest was served by my election. My party affiliation did not matter. In races where the outcome was clear (a safe seat with an incumbent, for example), they simply gave money to the expected winner regardless of party affiliation. However, they did not give money to those who actively opposed their bill.

The labor unions, in addition to contributing directly to my campaign, would contact their members in my district by mail or phone to make sure they voted and that they voted for me. Of course, they would also be pitching for other labor-endorsed candidates from president to coroner. This type of activity by unions and other membership groups, if confined to the membership of the organization, does not count under the law as a direct contribution to a candidate. The unions would also try to send volunteers to help with literature drops and mailings, and this is where the teachers did more.

PUBLIC FINANCING OF CAMPAIGNS

Watergate, the big bang of postwar American politics, shed light on the shadowy world of campaign money. Watergate prompted a nationwide call for campaign finance reform. In 1974 Congress passed the Federal Election Campaign Act Amendments, which were intended to regulate contributions and spending in federal political campaigns. Two years later, however, the rush to reform was checked by the U.S. Supreme Court in *Buckley* v. *Valeo*. This decision declared that limits on the amount a candidate (either the individual or the candidate's campaign) could spend violated the First Amendment guarantee of free speech. However, the Court did find the spending limits permissible for candidates who accepted public financing of their campaigns. In addition, the Court upheld limits that the 1974 law placed on the amount individuals and political action committees (PACs) could contribute to candidates.

Zeal for campaign finance reform at the federal level was mirrored at the state level. The Wisconsin legislature enacted public financing of campaigns in 1978. It was one of the first states to do so. No doubt, the Progressives applauded in their graves; in their view if the playing field were level, the best candidate would win, and good government would surely follow. Wisconsin also was one of three states (Wisconsin, Minnesota, and Hawaii) to include public funding for races for the state legislature. (Hawaii's law was flat surf from the word go because the public funding grant was $50; today it is an inconsequential $250.) Most of the other states restricted their laws to the race for governor and other statewide races, and a few provided some public funding to political parties.

Two simple, seemingly complementary, ideas were pursued by the Wisconsin legislature at the same time: contribution limits and spending limits. It would turn out that one was a square peg and the other a round hole.

The first idea was straightforward. The names of all contributors would have to be made public, and limits would be placed on the amount of money individuals could contribute to a candidate running for the state legislature. Political action committees would have similar limits. A further limit on PACs was a cap on the total amount of PAC funds a campaign could accept. For example, in a campaign for the Assembly, individuals could give $500 and a PAC could give $500, but the total of all PAC contributions could not exceed $4,500 in this race. These contribution limits, because they were so low, would pretty much ensure that no one individual or PAC could have undue influence, or, in less delicate terms, no one would be able to buy a candidate.

These contribution limits were not contingent on public financing. However, public financing was a compensation for these restrictions, as well as a means to help challengers compete with incumbents, who seemed to get all the money. In effect, "public finance" was envisioned as a pot of money that a candidate could dip into after raising a threshold amount of campaign money on his or her own from a number of contributors. Once a candidate claimed this "grant," however, certain restrictions applied. The candidate could not accept PAC money and had to agree to spending limits. The Buckley decision dictated this carrot-and-stick approach.

THE TAX CHECKOFF

The fight in the Wisconsin legislature was not over the essentials of the two ideas (contribution limits and spending limits) but over the mechanism to fund the pot of public finance money. Opponents of the public funding bill, those ideologically opposed to the use of public money for campaigns and incumbents who weren't about to hand lethal weapons to potential challengers, didn't have the votes to defeat the bill, and proponents couldn't win passage without some of them coming on board. So the scheme of the taxpayer checkoff was hatched as a way to move things along. Instead of simply adding funding for the cost of the grant to the state budget, legislators decided that one dollar would go into the pot when a taxpayer checked a box on the front page of the state income tax form.

The proponents of the bill, including me, wanted the check mark to mean the state would put a dollar in the pot from general tax revenue. The opponents of the bill wanted the check mark to mean that the income tax filer was adding a dollar to his or her tax liability. The opponents were no dummies when it came to taxpayers' behavior. They knew that only liberals and ministers would knowingly increase their taxes, and they predicted that the add-a-dollar plan would become an underfinanced law, abandoned when the post-Watergate clamor for campaign reform quieted. (After all, there was no scandal in Wisconsin. Wasn't the problem in Washington?)

The add-a-dollar faction won, and the bill was sent to the governor. He immediately vetoed the portion of the bill that would have added a dollar to a willing taxpayer's liability. The state ended up with the reformers' version: for each checkoff the state added a dollar to the public finance pot. This clever veto was like a practical joke on the deserving. In the Assembly big smiles were passed around like cigars as news spread of the governor's action. The opponents of the bill felt betrayed, and this double-cross, in their view, was not to be forgotten.

PUBLIC FUNDING IN PRACTICE

Wisconsin's new campaign finance law did make campaigns fairer fights. Challengers who could raise $1,000 from at least ten people (no person contributing more than $100) would receive from the state a sizable grant of $4,900. At first, Democrats generally opted in and Republicans, because of their philosophical problems with public financing, did not.

Under Wisconsin's public financing law, a candidate has until the primary election to reach the threshold in individual contributions required to qualify for public funding. One primary election night at a party organized to watch the election results, I stationed myself inside the doorway and asked each person entering (I knew most of them) to give me a small check made out to a specific Democratic candidate for the Assembly. This required a rapid-fire sales pitch to explain what I was doing and get them reaching for their checkbooks. Soon there was a whole separate line of party goers writing checks to candidates they did not know because it was a way to keep the Democrats in the majority. When enough was raised for one candidate, I started on the next. Then I started to collect checks with the payor left blank in order to be able to have some flexibility to give more to the big talkers, the candidates who never raised the money they claimed they would.

By 9:00 P.M. I had well over one hundred checks stuffed in my inside coat pocket, and I hustled up State Street to the Capitol two blocks away. Gathered there from various parts of the state were about a dozen candidates or their treasurers, milling about the staff office of the Democratic caucus. I distributed the checks so each would have enough money to reach the $1,000 threshold required to qualify for the grant.

The Republicans, feeling their minority status was setting in like arthritis, soon overcame their qualms about buying brochures with the public purse, and they started to employ the same strategy as the Democrats. For an election cycle or two the law worked pretty much the way it was hoped it would. Most candidates, even those in hotly contested open seats, took public funding, which meant they were also under the spending limit, and the contests against entrenched incumbents were less one-sided affairs, although the chances and the instances of the challenger winning remained slim, about the same likelihood as the Cubs winning their division. (Public financing was restricted to general elections.)

If challengers were running against a long-time incumbent in a safe seat, the race was no longer like a biplane chasing a jet that took off a day earlier. The spending limit was set high enough, $9,825 to begin with, and it was automatically increased at the rate of inflation, so adjustments to increased campaign costs in the future could be provided for without requiring the hurdle of a new update of the law every two years.

Political wisdom is insight derived from hindsight, and it is clear now that at the time it was in the self-interest of the two political parties (as they are manifested in the legislature) to employ public financing as part of a strategy where the goal never changes, and that is to try to win the winnable seats. It also worked because the spending limit was high. No incumbent or serious challenger was really disadvantaged by the limit, so taking public funds did not mean fighting with one hand tied behind your back. Did a different type of person run for or get elected to the legislature? No.

SPENDING LIMITS

In 1978 the spending limit of almost $10,000 for candidates for the Assembly who accepted public financing seemed high enough. However, the spending limit started to increase steadily because of the original law's provision for automatic indexing tied to the inflation rate, which at the time was very high. To hold down campaign spending, the reformers, including me, called for a repeal of the index. Without much thought it was jettisoned. The spending limit for an Assembly race was frozen at $17,250 unless and until the legislature decided to change it.

Within the blink of an eye, just one election cycle, the spending limit began to look dangerously low to incumbents, and more so to the contestants of both parties vying for a marginal seat. There was still an incentive to abide by the limit, however. The grant, which also grew according to an index (which was not repealed), remained a hefty amount. If one candidate opted out of public financing, the other candidate still got the grant, but the spending limit was lifted for both candidates. Thus, if you were the candidate opting out, you gave your opponent a gift of $7,763, a deficit you had to make up in order to get to the same starting line, and you unilaterally moved the finish line farther away by causing the spending limit to be lifted.

THE FAILURE OF A NOBLE EXPERIMENT

The first part of Wisconsin's campaign finance law required the disclosure of the names of those who gave a candidate more than twenty bucks, restricted cash contributions, and limited the size of individual and PAC contributions to campaigns. All of these reforms, which now seem so minimal and obvious, helped make a clean state cleaner. The other part of the 1978 law, spending limits, was a noble experiment that ultimately failed.

During the 1980s the value of a seat in the legislature increased dramatically because the margin of the Democratic majority decreased. When the public financing law was enacted, Democrats enjoyed close to a two-thirds majority in both the Assembly and the Senate. The public financing law lost its meaning for competitive races when the Democrat's majority in the Assembly slipped to 52-47. The stakes were too high (control of one house of the legislature) for many candidates to voluntarily abide by spending limits just because fair fights and political chivalry are honorable things. Furthermore, in the races in the marginal seats, the loss of the grant by the challenger, most often the Republican, was quickly replaced by PAC money.

The total of all PAC contributions that could be given to a campaign and the public finance grant were the same dollar amount. If you took the grant, you could take no PAC funds. If you did not take the grant, you could, in effect, replace it by raising PAC money. So the loss of the grant meant little given the reservoir of available PAC money and the little it took to reach the legal limit. The value of a seat in the legislature, because it meant party control, was worth more than the artificially low spending limit in the public finance law. It is like the difference between the official rate (the legal spending limit) and the black market rate (the spending needed to win). The black market rate is closer to the real value of the commodity.

One result of all of these gyrations was perverse. The candidates who regularly opted for public funding were incumbents in marginal seats. Challengers had to forgo spending limits in order to have a chance to unseat these incumbents, and the incumbents would get the public money as well as be relieved of spending limits. The incumbents could pat themselves on the back because they were not taking PAC money and rail at their opponents for not abiding by spending limits and smile all the way to the bank.

The last shovelful of dirt thrown on the grave of public financing came as a result of the stupid funding mechanism that had been invented to get the original bill passed. Fewer and fewer tax filers checked the public funding box on the front of their income tax return forms, and the grants started to be prorated. From a high of 12 percent, the share of Wisconsin tax filers who checked the box fell to only 10.4 percent in 1993. (In states where the checkoff means the filer pays an extra dollar in taxes, the participation rate, which was always low, is now less than 1 percent.)

The decline in the checkoff rate meant the public finance pot shrunk, which in turn meant a candidate would not know what the actual dollar amount would be until the number of candidates opting in was determined, and the prorating could be figured. Uncertainty over a big chunk of money is usually not the handmaiden of success when the stakes are high in a campaign. I finally stopped taking public funding in order not to reduce the size of the grant available to others, who were mostly Democrats.

In the end the law became like Humpty Dumpty: it could not be put back together again. Neither party wanted to try. The spending limit could not be raised because that would look bad to reformers and because it wasn't in the self-interest of incumbents, who were starting to realize how the low limit could work to their advantage. Moreover, there was no public pressure to "do something." The public may not have lost faith, but it certainly had lost interest. So we were stuck with a public grant that was dwindling and with spending limits that were unrealistically low.

I finally came to the conclusion that the spending limit was the wrong goal. Perhaps campaign spending in Wisconsin would have been lower if we had enacted only the contribution limits and the public funding and skipped spending limits altogether. Artificial limits are just that.[3]

Disclosure, contribution limits, and public funding are good things, and by themselves add up to a better system, a system that brings us closer to an essential American goal—more equality among the players. The laws can be made to work more effectively. Participation can be increased by manipulating the grant size and the spending limit. Participation in Minnesota went down when the spending limits and the grant size were not updated. The Wisconsin experience would have been echoed in Minnesota had that state not quickly raised the spending and grant limits and increased the checkoff from $2 to $5. There is no requirement in Minnesota that a candidate raise a matching amount to qualify for public funding, and the political parties receive money from the fund, which makes them even stronger.

The idea that money, "the mother's milk of politics," can be contained in a small saucer, or that any system of laws can take the corruption out of the chase for campaign cash, is unrealistic.

Placing artificially low prices on a product in great demand does not work. Maybe the "money is water" analogy is a guide. The campaign finance laws, including public funding, are like rain gutters. They do not stop rain from falling on a house, but they channel it away from the foundation so fundamental damage does not eventually occur.

POLITICAL ACTION COMMITTEES

There is a rubric in the bible of campaign finance reform that special interest money, usually not distinguished from PAC money, is bad. A political action committee is a common fund paid into by members of an interest group. The money collected is given out in contributions to candidates who tend to favor the general or specific interests of the group's members. Officers chosen by the group decide which candidates to sup-

---

[3] David Adamany, the architect of Wisconsin's campaign finance law, notes that campaign spending has not increased as much in Wisconsin as in other states. However, the spending increase for legislative races has been greater than for other offices in the state. He attributes this to more heated competition in more legislative districts than in the past—a good development.

port (the endorsement process). Take the AFL-CIO as an example. A small part of each member's union dues is automatically given to the union's PAC, unless the member specifically asks not to contribute, an act of initiative that is uncommon. This "negative checkoff" adds up to a lot of money because there are a lot of members in the union in the state, and because few members ask to be excluded from the program.

The teachers' union PAC is financed by automatic contributions of $12 per year. About 93 percent of the teachers participate in the PAC with the rest asking for and receiving a rebate of their contribution.

The public finance law diminished the influence of PACs in individual campaigns. Wisconsin has one of the lowest levels of PAC contributions to candidates of any state. A PAC can give a candidate only $500. No matter how general its interest or predictably partisan an interest group may be, if its PAC can give only $500 to a candidate, it will have less influence on that candidate than if its PAC could contribute $1,000 or $5,000.

Another consequence of Wisconsin's $500 PAC limit was that it made one PAC as good as the next. There are so many PACs around that if one doesn't give, another one will. If the dentists don't, the embalmers will; if the teachers don't, the beer distributors will; and the total amount of PAC funds allowed to be raised under the law will be quickly reached. So candidates now, at least all incumbents and all those running in marginal districts, know that they can easily raise this much PAC money, and it matters little which PAC actually provides the money. You just cash the checks as they arrive and send back the ones that come after the PAC pot is full.

Not all special interest money is PAC money, however. Take my old friends the chiropractors. They never did have a PAC. Instead they have a system whereby each chiropractor parcels out individual personal checks to the candidates targeted by the political arm of the Wisconsin Chiropractic Association. This allows the chiropractors to bundle their cash and, in a rain of envelopes, easily provide $5,000 to the favored candidate in an Assembly race (usually an incumbent who is a member or leader of the health, insurance, or budget committee).

The bankers showed they could write checks when a bill allowing interstate banking came along. Opposed to the bill, the big Wisconsin banks leaned on their board members, officers, and the customers they held hostage to credit, urging them to write personal checks to any incumbent of either party who was breathing. The big banks from Minnesota and New York that they were trying to stop fought back. They threw cash over the state line using the same method—personal checks targeted to supporters of the bill.

Next, to get around the PAC limits, conduits were invented. Groups would collect little checks from members, place the money in one account, and send one big check to the favored candidate along with a list of all the small-check contributors. Conduits were not contemplated when the campaign law was passed, and when they appeared it was hard to distinguish them from a PAC. (They looked and quacked like a PAC, so they must be a PAC.) The clever arrangement was hard to undo because it was legal. Conduits are now a mature branch of the campaign money tree.

Finally, like a swollen river that makes a new path, PACs circumvented the $500 limit on direct contributions to a candidate by funding their own campaigns on the candidate's behalf. These efforts paralleling a candidate's own campaign have become quite sophisticated. The most sophisticated, the independent expenditure efforts of the teachers' union, is explained in Chapter 9. Again, the *Buckley* decision protected these campaign expenditures on free speech grounds, and they are now very important in races for marginal seats.

PARTY RESOURCES

In some states the political party recruits candidates and provides campaign help and money. In other states the candidate for the legislature is pretty much on his or her own. But even then the party is important. People run and vote as Democrats or Republicans because of important personal reasons. They may vote Republican because they share the party's philosophy of less government. They may vote Democratic for historical reasons; they were young and desperate in the Depression, and it was Franklin Delano Roosevelt who cared and helped. Because of these party ties, candidates have a built-in block of voters who are on their side the minute they declare their candidacy.

The United States' winner-take-all political structure ensures a two-party system. But the two parties are weak, and this too is intentional. Selecting candidates to represent each party through a primary election does not restrict the voting decision to party members, and there is little in the way of endorsements to reward the loyal or sanction the wayward officeholder. Why? It is because state representatives and members of Congress have a wider constituency and a personal campaign apparatus that allows them to be relatively independent of the party.

The state parties are not powerful, for the above reasons, and because they have little money to offer a candidate. Wisconsin is a state with very weak political parties (although politics is very partisan), because of the open primary and the Progressives' tradition that says "party bosses" are bad. This is ingrained in the political culture and has caused both parties to refrain from even endorsing a preferred candidate running in a primary. In contrast, the Minnesota parties may be said to be strong because they endorse in primaries, and this endorsement is fought for because it is worth something in return: help and money.

In addition to being weak, state parties have a fairly narrow focus. They concentrate on statewide races and the presidential campaign at the state level. Local units of the state parties focus on the county courthouse, fighting to control the offices of clerk and sheriff and coroner. Races for the state legislature receive scant attention.

Because money needed to be raised and directed toward marginal seats in the Assembly, and because good candidates needed to be recruited to run in these districts, a new independent wing of the state's political parties was created: the Assembly Democratic Campaign Committee (ADCC) and the Republican Assembly Campaign Committee (RACC). Two similar committees were created in the state Senate. All of these committees, informally called caucus committees, are under the control of the party leadership. Out of self-interest, legislative leaders have become responsible for retaining or gaining control of their house in the legislature.

This is the chicken, and the egg, some would argue, was the legislative leader who started to raise money to give to other candidates so they would then support him for election or reelection to a leadership position. Speaker Willie Brown of California started out raising and disbursing money to Democrats running for the Assembly who pledged to vote for him for Speaker. He also did this in primary elections, supporting the Democrat in the field who, in turn, would support him. Speaker Brown now worries about keeping any flock of Democrats in the majority and fighting referendums designed to take power away from the legislature. The days of buying a pal and a vote for Speaker are long gone. Now the "caucus committee" or the "leadership committee" in all state legislatures is a mature machine with a single function: to recruit, staff, and fund candidates in marginal seats. The function is carried on for a single purpose: to retain or gain control of a house in the legislature.

As the Speaker, I was the chairman, chief fund raiser, and strategy maven of the Assembly Democratic Campaign Committee. Although raising and giving money to others once was a way for all state legislators to gain supporters, now it is the particular job of the Speaker or the minority leader. Furthermore, raising and shelling out this money does not even buy grateful followers because it tends to be given to challengers and they usually lose! As Minnesota's former Speaker Bob Vanasek put it:

> I can't give some dissident out there some money to shut him up, because it means we're not funding a race somewhere else that we can win. We can't give money to incumbents in safe seats. They don't get a dime. And the other thing going on is that the ones who are getting it

don't bother to thank you because there is now an expectation that they are going to get it. They know it.

If you are the Speaker or the leader of the state Senate, raising money for targeted seats is as much a part of your job as pounding the gavel to call the house to order. It is your responsibility to keep your party in the majority. The caucus campaign committee is the vehicle. It's your party.

RAISING THE ANTE

Money now flows to marginal seats in races for the state legislature throughout the country in a similar pattern. Money is directed to these races regardless of the qualifications of the candidate. It is given solely because the races will take place in marginal districts. One example is an Assembly race in northern Wisconsin in 1988.

How did this twenty-four-year-old who had not yet graduated from college and was living in a hardscrabble part of the far sticks with his mother raise $50,000 to challenge a long-time Democratic incumbent? It happened because his mother had the good sense to live in a district that was targeted. That's how. In this case the lad won. Ninety-one percent of his contributions of over $100, the bulk of his money, came from outside his district, mostly from one faraway zip code in a silk-stocking suburb of Milwaukee. Old-money Republican business people dipped into their personal cache of cash and gave it to this kid because it was the way, they were told, for the Republicans to gain control of the Assembly.

The care and coaching of this ambitious young candidate, and the planting, nurturing, and growing of that money tree was accomplished by the Republican Assembly Campaign Committee. The talented Republican leader, my friend Betty Jo Nelson, had targeted the right seats and had organized in brilliant fashion the selling of the plan and the method to assemble the cash, mostly from partisans. By supplementing their coffers, she wanted each of her targeted candidates to have a minimum of $50,000 to spend against the incumbent Democrat. (The spending limit at the time for an Assembly race was $17,250.)

I was on the other side, mostly playing catch-up, trying to raise money for the Democrats in marginal seats who were under assault. The Democrats survived and sported buttons on the first day of the next session that read, "Member $50,000 club." Having failed to make the Republican Party the majority party in the Assembly, Betty Jo fell on her sword by resigning as the minority leader, an act that had some ennobling quality but little necessity.

CAUCUS COMMITTEE ALLOCATIONS

How are the caucus committees organized? Where does the money come from? How are seats determined to be marginal and thus targeted? And how does the constant quest for money, which is always needed because the day after the last election is simply the first day of the next election, play itself out in the lawmaking process?

Like a PAC, the caucus campaign committee raises money to give to candidates it supports. In this case the money goes to Democrats or Republicans running for the legislature. However, the caucus campaign committee is really more like a political party. Legally considered adjuncts or arms of the state party, these committees have powers that PACs do not have. For example, they can give and take transfers of money from their party. But they are different than a political party in three ways. First, the only "members" are legislators (the members of the ADCC are the Democratic incumbents in the Assembly), and the officers are the partisan legislative leaders. Second, the money is spent only on races for one office, the state legislature, and the only candidates the committees care about are those running in marginal seats. Third, their sole interest is in retaining or gaining majority control in their respective house in the legislature.

One of the reasons for the rise of legislative campaign committees in states is the inability of the two political parties to raise money. The legislative campaign committee can raise money because there are people and groups interested in the public policy decisions being made by the legislature. Regardless of who eventually gets the money, the contributor knows that the money is given to the legislative leaders, and they are the ones who will set the agenda and control the flow of legislation.

There is little discretion as to where the money goes. A targeted district is one that is considered marginal. The first step in this determination is the history of the partisan voting behavior in the *legislative* races in that district. If this average figure shows, for example, that the Republican usually wins with 54 percent of the vote (or, conversely, if the Democrat can expect at least 46 percent of the vote), the district is within the margin where either party could realistically win. The partisan voting behavior for other races within this district, such as those for president and governor, are not factored into the decision.

Districts within this 46 to 54 percent margin are then ranked in order of importance, and a list of targeted seats results. Districts where an incumbent will not be on the ballot (open seats) go to the top of the list. Districts where an incumbent won but with less than 54 percent of the vote are next on the list. The bottom third of the list is determined more intuitively. For example, if an incumbent has always won by 54 percent, he probably will again. However, if this time, unlike previous elections, this same incumbent has raised little money and hasn't sent the usual 5,000 highway maps into his district, it might mean his guard is down and he is ripe for a challenge. Also on the list, farther down, are the open seats that are not too far outside the 46 to 54 percent margin. The list is the same for both parties.

The money needed to help finance the candidates on the targeted list must be raised systematically and continuously, and it is the job of the legislative leader.

ASSESSING CAUCUS CAMPAIGN COMMITTEES

Because they are like political parties, and because competitive political parties are an important check on abuse of power in government, the good things about caucus campaign committees more than outweigh the bad. Today the big political money tends to go to or through the caucus campaign committee, rather than to the individual candidate, historically the incumbent. This means that whatever the money might buy is purchased from the legislative leadership—a less corrupting focal point because it has to do more with access than influence. The competing demands on a leader—inside (from the members of the legislature) and outside (from pressure groups and the press)—act as a natural check against the leader giving in, or giving up, or giving any one thing to any one group.

The committees also redistribute special interest money in a healthy although indiscriminate way. For example, a PAC for the telephone company gives to the ADCC, which in turn gives money to candidates on the targeted list. A targeted candidate may favor reducing pay phone calls to a nickel because he believes the telephone company is a monopoly with rigged prices. Furthermore, this dangerous radical, from the phone company's point of view, may be challenging the incumbent who has been the best friend of phone companies since Alexander Graham Bell.

In this way caucus campaign committees channel special interest money into the purchase of competitive races for the legislature, something that is a presumed good. Another benefit is that the caucus campaign committees help strengthen the political parties because it is in their self-interest to do so. A considerable amount of money, generated by the caucus committee, now flows to the party to help make sure races above and below the legislator on the ticket are also competitive in order to help the candidate for the legislature.

The bad in all this is that these committees are not replacements for strong political parties. Although they channel money, their feeding requires an escalating amount of money. Most money elsewhere in the system also has a partisan cast to it—those who give it feel their interest would be served better by a member of one party rather than the other. However, much of the money given to the caucus committees by special interests is chasing a particular outcome in the legislature, and it matters little if those who make the decision are Republicans or Democrats.

MONEY AT WORK

It's easy to ask for money if you are the Speaker. All conversations are about the same. The road builders were big contributors to the caucus committees, and their lobbyist would receive several calls a week. If I called, and you were in the room, this is what you would hear:

> SPEAKER: Jim, this is Tom. How are you today?
> LOBBYIST: Quite good. Thank you for asking Mr. Speaker. How can I help you?
> SPEAKER: The campaign committee is having a fundraiser the first night of session, right after we adjourn, and I hope a few of your clients can attend.
> JIM: I assume it is at the Upper Crust.
> SPEAKER: That is right. We are trying to raise $30,000 at this event, and I hope the road builders can help. At the last event I think your guys kicked in $5,000. Do you think that's in the ballpark for this time?
> JIM: I don't know. But I will do what I can, and I will see you on the twenty-fifth.

The asking for and giving of campaign money has its own language and is accompanied by a lot of winking, blinking, and nodding. Rarely is any quid pro quo discussed. First, this is illegal, both for the lobbyist to ask and for the legislator to give. Second, the legislature is as open as a sieve; there are no secrets. Some legislators and lobbyists, however, go close to the line of illegality in order to try to gain an accomplice and an edge.

The Speaker's office is not large. It is square and a brass chandelier hangs dead in the middle. The large window faces North, and even a cloudy day brings a glinting light that is harsh. There is one green leather couch and chair of the classic style you might think would fit in a London men's club. Against the wall opposite the couch stands an oak roll-top desk, one of the last of the original pieces made in Milwaukee. It was moved into the new building built after the fire in 1916 destroyed the old capitol. There is another table-like desk in front of it that is more functional. Like a captive, I could predictably be found behind the table desk.

One day as I slouched in the desk chair with the phone lodged between my shoulder and ear, the lobbyist for the chiropractors walked in and sat down on the couch below the portrait of Fighting Bob LaFollette. A shady character, by Wisconsin standards, with no finesse, the lobbyist looked at me and held up two fingers on his left hand and all five on his right hand and mouthed the word "thousand." He walked out before I could get off the phone. I found him later and told him no and never to do that again. He was the sort who would recount this "meeting" to his clients as proof of his clout and an indication of their obligation. The message was that if the chiropractic bill passed, I could count on $25,000 for the campaign committee. This was illegal and dangerous because the bill always passed and this time the stakes were higher because the new governor, unlike his predecessors, would sign the bill.

MONEY AND CONTROL

Many tributaries join in the river of cash that is spent on legislative races when the stakes are high. Consider this example from April 1993, when a special election was held for three vacant seats in the state Senate. (One Democratic state senator had been elected to the U.S. Senate, another had been elected to the U.S. House, and a third vacancy had been created when the Republican governor appointed another Democratic senator, who was flexible in his party loyalty, to a cushy state job at a high salary.) These three vacancies left a 15-15 partisan tie in the Senate. The party that won two of the three seats would gain majority control. All three districts were winnable by either party, and all six candidates were experienced. Four were members of the Assembly, one held a county office, and one was a former member of the legislature.

Because party control of one house of the legislature was at stake, the prospects of several interest groups would improve or dim based on the outcome. If the Republicans won, organized labor, particularly the teachers' union, would be on the defensive. The big losers would be the trial lawyers. Democrats did not support a cap on jury trial awards for medical malpractice and product liability, and Republicans did. So teachers, labor, and the trial lawyers lined up with the Democrats. Lining up behind the Republicans were the traditional business groups and doctors, insurance companies, and others interested in caps on awards in trials. This rough division of loyalty was natural and already existed.

All three races were decided by close margins. The Republicans won two of the three vacant seats and took control of the Senate. The one Democrat who won, Joe Wineke, had been a member of the Assembly and had served on the Finance Committee. When asked to characterize where his money came from, he had a tidy answer: "I learned, when push comes to shove in a critical election, people go home. They are going to dance with the one that brought them." His money, as well as that of the other five candidates, came mostly from those who wanted to see a Democrat elected rather than a Republican, or vice versa.

MONEY AND ITS SOURCES

The spending by these six candidates for the state Senate ranged from a low of $125,000 to a high of $290,000. Where did the money come from? Let us look at the contest between Joe Wineke and Jonathan Barry, a former Democratic member of the Assembly who had switched parties. Both Wineke and Barry were young, articulate, successful, and ideologically moderate. In fact, they agreed on some important issues like abortion.

Neither candidate accepted PAC money! Each candidate raised around $200,000; mostly from individual contributors. The maximum legal contribution by an individual was $1,000. Joe Wineke's thousand-dollar contributors were trial lawyers. He raised a total of $38,000 from them in individual contributions of $500 to $1,000.

The rest of Wineke's money came mainly from "known contributors": people who had recently given money to other Democrats. This money, which would total close to $100,000 by the campaign's end, was raised through mailings and phone calls. Russ Feingold, the state senator who vacated the seat to run successfully for the U.S. Senate, signed the three most successful fundraising letters. This state Senate district included 150,000 people and spanned the city of Madison and rural areas to the West. Most of Wineke's small donations came from in and around this area, and he estimates that he personally knew 40 percent of those who gave him a check.

The groups whose interests would not be particularly affected by a change in party control gave money to both Wineke and Barry, with a little more going to Wineke because he would still be in the Assembly even if he lost the Senate race. The home builders, for example, gave equal amounts to both candidates. (The occupations of contributors have to be listed if the check exceeds $100.) There was one exception. The doctors ended up officially supporting Wineke because their political arm voted to do so after the Wineke campaign stacked the endorsement meeting with local doctors friendly to him. (It is a game of inches!) It didn't take a brain surgeon to figure out that because of Joe's status as a member of the Finance Committee in the majority party he would be more powerful in the legislature if he lost than if he won.

Jonathan Barry raised his money pretty much the same way. The large contributors were the "who's who" of the local and state business community, especially those connected with manufacturing. Smaller donations came primarily from "known contributors" to Republicans, and they were tapped through mailings and telephone solicitations.

The unions—the AFL-CIO, the United Auto Workers, the teachers, the Teamsters, the public employee unions, and others—all chipped in from their individual PACs to fund a new cooperative PAC (Wisconsin

Citizens for Responsive Government). This PAC spent almost $300,000, mostly on TV ads for the three Democrats or against the Republicans. The Republican leader in the Senate quickly organized a conduit (Majority GOP) and funded it to the tune of almost $300,000 from individual contributors who could afford to write a big check without transferring money from another account. The labor PAC spent money on behalf of the three Democratic candidates, and the Republican conduit gave money to the three GOP candidates. Thus, one was a PAC because spending on behalf of candidates was the purpose, and one was organized as a conduit because getting money to candidates was the purpose.

The two caucus campaign committees in the state Senate, the PAC-like organizations described earlier, each spent about $115,000 (in direct contributions to the candidates and donations to the political parties). Now here is where things get a bit tricky. Since the caucus committees are treated as adjuncts to their respective party, they can transfer money to the party in unlimited amounts, and vice versa. The Senate Democratic Campaign Committee gave money to the party for voter ID activity. Voters who identify themselves as Democrats are found, and this list is given to the Democratic candidates so they can be sure and ask them for money and remind them to vote on election day.

This ID effort, which is done by knocking on doors in targeted areas and conducting telephone polls, is called party building. Only a minimal amount of this money must be counted in the expenditure totals of individual candidates. It was designed, in a reform of the presidential election laws, to be a party-building loophole. The loophole works. The result has been twofold: the party has become an umbrella organization for individual campaigns, and the party checkbook has become a good place to launder campaign money directed at targeted races.

In addition to the money received from the Senate Democratic Campaign Committee for the ID effort, the Democratic Party of Wisconsin spent another $110,000 for the two-out-of-three election. The Republicans do it a little differently, but they spent about the same amount. Who gives money to the parties for this activity? For the Democrats it is the union PACs, and other PACs associated with the party, and the trial lawyers. The Republican Party gets its money from PACs traditionally sympathetic to its cause and from known contributors of big checks.

Because the stakes were high—control of the state Senate—the "tributaries" mentioned earlier soon flooded the river with nearly $2 million (the spending total from all sources for all three races).

BALANCING THE BOOKS

Campaign laws can regulate donation amounts, dictate disclosure, and help level the field for the challenger. PAC spending limited in one way (direct contributions to a candidate) will continue in another guise (independent campaign expenditures by PACs on behalf of the candidate). There will also be unintended consequences that are beneficial. In Wisconsin all candidates must find a large number of individual contributors to give small donations in order to finance a winning campaign. (Joe Wineke's campaign listed almost 2,000 contributors.) This is good and it happened because of the limits on PACs and the limit on large personal contributions. However, campaign finance laws have had unintended negative consequences as well. Many of the contributors of large sums are the same people writing conduit checks, or the same individuals participating in "targeted giving" organized by special interests. In another system they would give to their PAC. Limits on spending by PACs tend to be compensated for by increased donations by individuals. Consequently, disclosure of the identity of the special interest is lost—an unintentionally bad result.

State legislatures and the Congress can pass laws to plug holes in the dike as money is discovered to be seeping through, but a more likely avenue for success is to channel the money so it can be seen and counted. Public financing can play a role, and can have a real impact in increasing competition, but this modest promise of what it can do should not be allowed to inflate into a religion that guarantees salvation.

Laws can write the rules of the political money game, but laws cannot dictate the stakes, set the odds, or limit the amount people are willing to bet when the stakes are high and there is a lot to lose and a lot to gain.

WHAT DOES MONEY BUY?

There is personal money, partisan money, public finance money, and special interest money.

A candidate can count on personal money (money from friends and relatives) simply because he or she asks and they want to help. This money is important in races for the legislature. It is the seed money. It buys little in the way of influence because it is not given for that purpose.

Partisan money is given by people and groups whose interest is served better by electing a Democrat rather than a Republican, or vice versa. This is money the candidate expects to receive and the contributors have budgeted to give. It buys predictability. Contributors of partisan money want Democrats to act like Democrats and Republicans to act like

Republicans once in office. This is tacitly understood by both the givers and the takers.

Public finance pays the entry fee for those who otherwise wouldn't have a chance in a campaign. They won't get much partisan or special interest money, so the public finance grant buys some competition in campaigns where there otherwise would be little. It also enables some candidates to substitute money with no strings attached for money with strings attached. Many people in politics don't want a pocketful of IOUs; public finance cuts a lot of strings.

Special interest money is given to buy access and influence. For example, the contributor to the caucus campaign committee buys access to the leadership. The contributor doesn't buy a vote from anyone, let alone purchase a guaranteed victory, but it is the fee that will, in all likelihood, get its horse entered in the race.

This means that the groups that give to the caucus committee, either through their PAC or by bigger personal checks from the principals, have a presence in the mind of the leader. They influence seemingly humdrum decisions like which speaking engagement to accept and who the legislative leader, rather than his or her aide, should see on a busy day. At the end of the session, when the pile of equally bad ideas has climbed to yardstick height, the leader might pick the bad idea of the contributor to debate rather than any of the others in the stack. More likely, the idea, bad or good, of his competitor will not be placed on the top of the pile.

Most political money is given for the purpose of preventing bad things from happening to a group, or for preserving the status quo. It is much easier for leaders to prevent bills from passing, than it is for them to cause bills to be passed. Most groups and people with power and money in our society have gotten what they want by this time. Their interest is to try to protect it from competitors, whether they be ideological or business rivals.

The truest thing I can say about special interest money is that it is mainly given to buy the status quo. Ideas, elections, reapportionment, more minorities and women serving, change of party control—all these things produce change in a legislature. And the threat of change is what special interest money seeks to minimize. Special interest groups mostly give money so something bad doesn't happen to them in the legislature.

Legislative Leadership: Apprenticeship in the School of Chaos

The bright Way seems dim. The forward Way seems backward. The level Way seems bumpy.[1]

Lao Tzu

As Speaker of the Assembly for eight years, every day was different. On some days I was like the teacher in front of the classroom. I was the font of real knowledge, and I decided what we did during the day, including when we took recess. On other days I was like someone in front of a firing squad who is fumbling with his blindfold and last cigarette in order to buy time. A leader's goal is to have more days like the former than the latter.

Knowing the history of the institution, which can come only from serving and observing, is essential, if for no other reason than it allows the leader to avoid mistakes that were made in similar circumstances in the past. Leaders get in trouble because they are poor learners or because they think things didn't work before because a predecessor lacked the right stuff, and they try the failed strategy a second time. The leaders who get in real trouble are the ones who believe effectiveness comes with the mere fact of being put in charge.

As I matured in my tenure, I still had days in front of the firing squad, but by then I had learned to fumble with my blindfold with such alacrity and aplomb that I appeared to be in control. I got to the point where I could try risky things, and if they didn't work it still looked like part of a plan. One success led to another. Even in the midst of risk and chaos, I

[1] Lao Tzu, *Tao Te Ching: The Classic Book of Integrity and the Way*, translated, annotated, and with an afterword by Victor H. Mair (New York: Bantam Books, 1990), 7.

became secure among my followers; the Democrats became believers, and believers are good followers. My practice of going the unlikely way, and of doing by seeming not to do, began to be called by my colleagues Zen leadership.

APPRENTICESHIP

What looked to others like a gift for leadership did not come to me on a visit to a mountain top. I was trained for the job. The training began in February 1973, just after the start of the session, when I was hired as a speech writer for the sixty-seven Democrats in the Wisconsin Assembly. I had never written a speech in my life, but Dick Randall, the staff director for the Democratic caucus, was looking for a not-too-liberal type for a little balance, and he liked my résumé. I had been in the army, and I had served as a military policeman, the item that really caught his attention. In fact, being drafted and serving as an MP at Fort Bliss in El Paso (not one Viet Cong came across the Rio Grande River during my stay) did not make me more conservative. Nevertheless, I fit in and found out I could actually write a speech. Speech writing is, more or less, writing down how other people talk at their most lucid.

I wrote speeches for every member on every subject imaginable. If legislators wanted to close prisons or if they wanted the death penalty for jaywalking, I would give them good rhetoric and the facts on their side. Six of us sat in a big room churning out press releases, memos, and letters, as well as speeches. In our boiler room there was a "squawk box" so we could hear the debate from the Assembly chamber two floors above. It was like Berlitz class for learning the legislative process. By listening to the debates, I got to know the members. I would try to write speeches in their speaking style that were true to their philosophies (ranging from socialist to libertarian), and I used examples meaningful to their districts.

A legislature has a rhythm based on its history. Listening on the squawk box taught me a lot. Like a pupil in school, I moved on to specialized study after two years when the Speaker, Norm Anderson from Madison, hired me as his staff person. (Yes, the staff was only me and able secretary Pat Cornwell.)

When I entered the Assembly as a member two years later, it was often said, not totally in jest, that I now had less power than I had as Norm's aide. Then my staff duties had ranged from assigning parking spaces to doing the first draft of committee appointments, including appointing the chairs. I became the sounding board for members who had ideas and the confessor for those who had gripes. I had the run of the place, like the boss's son, and was sought out by both sides to be told of the latest palace intrigue. I was a witness of events and also a student. This was especially true when it came to the meetings of the Assembly Democrats in caucus.

THE PARTY CAUCUS

The word *caucus* refers to the members of a political party in one house of a legislature. (For example, all the Republicans in the Assembly are the Republican caucus). A caucus can also be a meeting of those members. When the Democrats in the Assembly met as a group to talk about strategy, they would be in a caucus. (A caucus caucuses in a caucus room.)

In the Assembly the caucuses were held in the North hearing room, a large, windowless, two-story room on the second floor. It was like a vault in an old-money bank. The doors were ornate gates of iron bars, and the chairs were upholstered in black leather. The lighting was bad, as was the smoke-filled air.

The caucuses were closed to the press and everyone else who was not a member except for me, the Speaker's aide. I was an audience of one watching a company of good actors bring to life the drama, pathos, and comedy of a brilliant playwright. Some days it was statesmanship of the highest order with oratory to match. Some days it was comedy with clever word play followed by slapstick. And some days it was hate-filled drama, the kind that could cause a trigger to be pulled. On these days if the worst thing you saw was a grown man cry, you were lucky. Harvey Dueholm, a beloved veteran member of the Assembly with an earthy way of cutting to the quick, often said, "The difference between a caucus and a cactus is that the cactus has the pricks on the outside."

In the caucus room I learned a lot about the psychology of leadership. Three things will help make a leader effective. First, the leader is expected to direct the group. However, the leader must possess and exude the serenity of one who understands it is natural that he or she be in charge. Second, the leader must learn to state the obvious because important things may be obvious only to the leader. If it is time to give up, the leader must recount the events that have led to this conclusion, including all the paths taken along the way that turned out to be dead ends. Third, the leader must know when to pose the question to his or her caucus. If you keep people in a room long enough, they will eventually make a decision. Members of a jury usually can't come out of the room until they all agree on a verdict. Therefore, the choices they are given by the judge are pretty important.

THE CAMPAIGN FOR A LEADERSHIP POST

To become a legislative leader (such as Speaker or majority leader or minority leader) you must run for the position. This is obvious. But not so obvious, even to many legislators, is that the campaign for such a post is in itself a lesson in leadership.

During the campaign you learn a lot because your colleagues tell you about their plans and goals. Running for a leadership position is also a teaching experience: you tell your colleagues of your plans and goals. And it is a humbling experience because everyone is telling you about your faults even as they extol your virtues. The comments range from the subtle ("You are doing a good job where you are. Who will take your place? What will we do with Charley if you defeat him?") to the brutal ("You have opposed every bill I proposed, and the last thing we need is another Dane County liberal in leadership. Get lost.").

You might think that if someone has campaigned for the legislature and won, he or she would be ambitious enough to then campaign for a leadership position in the legislature. This is not the case. In fact, few seek to be leaders, and these few tend to run for leadership spots throughout their tenure. Most of them, at least half, do eventually get elected. In the campaign for a leadership post, you ask your colleagues for their votes one at a time. This is part of the apprenticeship expected of potential leaders. Each conversation is a part of a puzzle. If you were listening and have a bit of the artist's eye, you can see the big picture, one of the things necessary to be an effective leader. Thus, a personal history develops between you and each legislator of your party.

Leadership elections are secret ballot affairs. Shortly after the November elections and before the start of the next session, each caucus convenes to choose its leaders. Each member is given a blank slip of paper to write the name of his or her choice for Speaker, for example. One slip of paper is given for each leadership position. After the members have folded their papers securely, like notes passed in grade school, the ballots are collected and counted; a representative of each candidate watches the tally. If no one gets a majority, the one receiving the fewest votes is dropped. Blank pieces of papers are handed out again, and the process is repeated. The winner is announced but not the vote count. However, the counters and the watchers soon whisper this information to the press, and it appears in the newspapers the next day.

The first who are culled out in leadership races are the ones who can't count. The losers, like Candidate A who is quoted below, are invariably surprised.

CANDIDATE A: I hope to get your vote for Speaker.

COLLEAGUE: You know I would like nothing better than to see you become Speaker.

If Candidate A counts this colleague as a vote, he will probably lose. Candidate B, on the other hand, is better at addition.

CANDIDATE B: Can I count on your vote for Speaker?

COLLEAGUE: We have been friends for a long time.

CANDIDATE B: That sounds like a pretty sound yes. Can I put your name down on my list?

COLLEAGUE: I would rather this be between you and me.

CANDIDATE B: You swing a lot of weight in the caucus, and you know if people think you're for the other guy, I've got trouble. I don't have to tell you that a lot follow your lead.

COLLEAGUE: You have plenty of votes. Everybody knows I'm for you.

CANDIDATE B: I know that, but A is telling everyone you told him to his face that you would like to see him Speaker. That's hurting me. Look I'll put your name down. I won't show it to my team for an hour. I'll just tell my wife; she asked about you. And if you change your mind, call. After all we have been through, that's fair. I'm asking you because it means a lot to me. I'm within two votes of nailing this down. It's important to me that you're on board right now. It could mean the other vote. Deal?

COLLEAGUE: OK. Put it down, but you owe me one.

CANDIDATE B: I won't forget.

When I had a name on my list, it was a sure vote. I had witnessed my dad many times stay at a farmer's kitchen table until after midnight, working the arithmetic, making the deal sweeter if needed to get the farmer's signature in his order book, and when that happened it was over. If I got a name on my list, a line was crossed, and regardless of the subtleties of the mating dance that was involved in asking for a vote, I knew that person would vote for me.

ASKING A COLLEAGUE FOR A VOTE

Asking a colleague for a vote is the most serious thing there is in the legislature. If it is granted, the giver has a request of equal significance in the bank. If it is denied, it's like refusing to lend five bucks to your sister. You would feel bad, and she would be devastated. So you don't ask unless it's needed, and you are willing to sign a blank IOU. The Speaker asking for a vote is like a mother asking a grown son for a small favor. You know you owe, and you know she wouldn't ask if it wasn't important, even if it seems a small request. So the leader, especially the Speaker, must know how to ask and when to ask because the answer will almost certainly be yes.

It is the effective leader who can do most things without asking, without promising a favor or making a threat, and that is the preferred way. However, it is the campaign for the job that teaches a leader how to ask and how to distinguish a yes from a no. And it is the campaign that teaches the leader how to get a vote.

The decision to support one colleague instead of another for a leadership post can be based on many seemingly logical reasons. These include ideology, geography, gender, race, past favors (such as help raising money), prospects of future favors (such as committee assignments), and even whether the person is good on TV. But these reasons are not important considerations when compared with friendship.

Your friends are your classmates. Your friends are the ones you serve with on a committee. Your friends are the ones who support your stupid amendment so you don't look so stupid. Your friends are the ones whom you help and the ones who help you. The members of a legislature are all in the same outfit. They passed the same initiation to get there, but it's the ones in your unit, your friends, that will be in your corner in a leadership race. That's the base.

Your friends become the lieutenants in the campaign. One is the campaign manager. He or she usually has the only other clipboard with "the list" of the committed, the leaners, the ones lost to the other side, and the few who are truly undecided. The process is straightforward. The candidate canvasses for votes and also asks others (who may have some pull with someone who won't commit) to call on your behalf. This usually includes friends who are not legislators. It may be a former legislator who is respected. It may be a mutual friend who is enough of an insider to know the patter appropriate from one outside of the fraternity. It is seldom a lobbyist, unless the person is a former colleague. People such as labor leaders or the governor or one of his coterie are pressed into service at the candidate's peril because their presence in the race implies that the candidate may be loyal to some constituency other than the group. Furthermore, your opponent would call the newspaper the next day, and you would be branded "labor's person" or the "governor's person." Anything like this, that may call the candidate's loyalty to the caucus or to the institution into question, could easily be the kiss of death.

Finally, there are those who simply won't commit, and to be safe they are given to the other candidate. Very few remain up for grabs. Usually they dislike both candidates.

WINNING OVER AN UNDECIDED COLLEAGUE

When I ran for majority leader, I was one vote short on the morning of the vote. I had one possibility left, a colleague I had openly not admired, who had not committed to my opponent for the same reason. Twenty minutes before the caucus was to begin, I went to his office and asked him to nominate me. I told him this last-minute public profession of his support would be the difference, and the others would know that he had held the grave question in the balance and had gone my way. I all but said that I would owe my election to him. This stuff was an arrow right to the bull's-eye of his ego. He was one who thought his manner and ponderous moralizing made him like a lord in the place, while the rest of us thought him more like the butler in the service of a pair of well-known lobbyists, whose clients were not orphans and widows.

His nominating speech was a doozy. The other candidates were nominated by their best friends or senior members of the caucus. Then it was my race and my turn. As the self-styled squire rose to speak on my behalf, all eyes turned to me. Each eye had a raised eyebrow above it. After listing my faults and my slights of him, which he seemed to have catalogued by subject area, he said: "Despite these things, I am supporting Tom for the job, and I expect this to help him grow as a person." I won by two votes. My count had been on target.

AN ATTEMPT TO DETHRONE THE SPEAKER

It was during the session that I was elected majority leader that I learned the lessons of leadership at the graduate level. On November 10, 1980, Ed Jackamonis was chosen by the Democrats in the postelection caucus to be the Speaker for a third term. He won by one vote over Majority Leader Gary Johnson, a disgruntled liberal who had teamed up with the conservatives in the caucus in an attempt to unseat the abrasive Jackamonis and end the liberal faction's decade-long dominance of policy and key committee chairmanships.

Two weeks later a member of the caucus who it was known had voted for Jackamonis was declared a loser of his election in a recount. Was he an ineligible voter? This wasn't the only controversy that swirled around the bitter fight between the factions for control of the Speaker's office. On one of the paper ballots in the not-so-secret caucus vote, a member scribbled what could only be deciphered as "Jackahonson." The vote was awarded to Ed. This round was a draw between the conservatives and the liberals.

Things might have bumped along for a while, but Ed decided, even while his throne still wobbled, to be vindictive rather than magnanimous. He exiled Johnson to a nothing committee and stripped Tom Hauke, the leader of the conservatives, of his chairmanship. Their response was to try to unseat Jackamonis. Jackamonis did not exile Hauke and Johnson until he had been safely elected Speaker, so another vote for Speaker in the Democratic caucus was not an option. Therefore, they plotted with the Republicans and the Democrats they could lure into their camp. As majority leader, I found myself in the middle of this battle. I had the regimental flag, but the regiment was split in two, the sides facing each other with rifles ready to fire.

An Unlikely Leader

About another Speaker it once was said, "Many did not know he had a glass eye, but if you looked closely you could tell because that was the eye with just a drop of human kindness in it." Many thought Ed lacked even that.

Ed Jackamonis came from a working-class family in New Britain, Connecticut, and was graduated with high honors from Northeastern University in Boston. He came to the University of Wisconsin for his master's degree and settled at the university's two-year center in Waukesha to teach political science and work on his Ph.D. Waukesha was then a rather sleepy city in a very Republican-voting suburban county not too far west of Milwaukee.

Ed always said that he was surprised to end up as a leader of the antiwar movement in Waukesha. What he meant, and what he knew, was that he didn't have the personality that inspired followers. But a leader of a cause, who grants no gray areas between right and wrong, does not have to have that welcome-wagon-lady personality that most politicians seem to have or are able to display at will. Ed was elected in 1970 to the Wisconsin Assembly, another arena where the fight against the war in Vietnam and the rotten culture that could tolerate such a travesty was taking place.

Ed was first elected Speaker pro tem (the deputy Speaker) partly because he knew the rules, something that was very important in the 1970s because the minority leader, John Shabaz, could occasionally tie the joint in knots with parliamentary nit-picking. One day it dawned on Ed to read a rule literally. Under the rules, a day had to pass between voting on a bill the first time and voting for the final passage (second reading and third reading). For example, if the first vote was on the legislative calendar for October 1, the vote on passage couldn't occur until we reached the calendar for October 3. Since the minority could delay at will, calendars were never finished on time, and the Assembly could be weeks or months behind. Votes on unimportant and important bills could depend on the wish of the minority Republicans.

One day Ed burst into the Speaker's office and said, "Let's interpret the rule to mean the actual date, not the date on our stupid calendars!" The Speaker did, and the Democrats then controlled the timing of votes. Ed gained the mystique of the one who cut through the Gordian knot, and it probably gave him the margin needed to be elected Speaker when Norm Anderson was unexpectedly defeated in the primary election of 1976.

MY PREVIOUS EXPERIENCE

My previous experience as the Speaker's aide, and my four short years as a legislator in the Assembly, did not prepare me for my role as negotiator between the factions when Tom Hauke and Gary Johnson decided to try to dump Ed. I had been elected majority leader by two votes, defeating Tom Hauke, who ran as one-half of a team with Johnson. In January, when the new legislature was sworn in, it would be the start of only my third term. However, it was already the third time I had run for a leadership position in the caucus.

I was accurately described by the press as an "outspoken liberal," but if I represented anything, it was the first and second termers, a group of bright young baby boomers who were in politics to change the world right now, and they had no intention of waiting around to gain influence. My elevation to the post of majority leader was the first tangible evidence of our ascendancy. I had also garnered the votes of all but one of the ten newly elected Democrats. Of the incoming freshmen, only Wally Kunicki from Milwaukee's South side had voted for Tom Hauke.

I was not new to leadership. I had been the leader of the new Young Turks and had fought many a losing fight on behalf of our version of truth and justice. We met as the "Tuesday Club" to plot the future and chat like insiders about things we assumed insiders chatted about, but mostly we met for the intrigue of it and for the delicious knowledge that the others wondered what we were doing. We met on Tuesday nights at the Fess Hotel, the equivalent of our tree house, and we invited gossipy or newsworthy guests in order not to be above suspicion. One memorable night we invited the Speaker. We talked about public policy, and he listened, while glaring at us through the smoke of his ever-present Bensen & Hedges Extra Long.

MY STRATEGY TO SAVE THE SPEAKER

I knew from the beginning that, no matter what, I should not allow another vote for Speaker. Ed must stay, or the minority would be in control. This had to be the end result, regardless of what happened in the meantime. Agony and chaos followed.

Chaos has gotten a bad rap. Out of chaos comes order. Thus, I would learn, if you seek a new order, foment chaos. The trick is to get the desired outcome. When a leader is experienced, he or she can leave, in order to let things fall apart, and then put them together in a more preferable way.

My strategy was to do nothing. Hauke finally said, yes, he would make a motion for a new vote for Speaker, but this type of procedural motion could be made only on a certain day and at a certain order of business on the calendar. It would take a two-thirds vote, which neither side could muster, to move to the vote sooner or to delay it once it was presented.

It became obvious that the thing to do was to stay out of floor session, or at least never get to that point on the calendar when Hauke could make his motion. This meant that each day we would convene the session, hear a prayer, recite the pledge, and then the Democrats would repair to a caucus to yell at each other until exhaustion and alcohol would allow us to fizzle into adjournment late in the evening. But that would be one more day a vote was not taken that would allow the Republicans to choose the Speaker.

The first thing that was clear to all of us, save perhaps Ed, was that Gary Johnson and Tom Hauke could not be expected to twiddle their thumbs for two years on minor committees. Ed had named Johnson, former majority leader and Finance Committee chair, to be the chair of the Tax Exemptions Committee, a lowly committee that on a good day might consider whether exempting Christmas trees from the sales tax had anything to do with the separation of church and state. Hauke, the former chair of the powerful committee with jurisdiction over insurance companies and medical malpractice, was also demoted, becoming a mere member of the committee he had formerly chaired. Gary and Tom's supporters were not sent to "Committee Siberia" by Ed, but they ended up very close to the border.

The second thing that was clear, especially to the veteran Democrats, was that this was another round, perhaps a decisive round, in the ongoing ideological fight between the liberals and the conservatives in the Democratic caucus. The battle had been going on since 1970 when the Democrats gained the majority and were in a position to push the programs of then-governor, Patrick Lucey.

Figuratively speaking, he attempted to shoot an archduke just about every day he was in office. If you were comfortable with the status quo, he had a proposal that would make you uncomfortable. He got a lot accomplished, and the liberal Democrats were his willing foot soldiers, but the conservatives were asked to take one political bullet in the chest after another and received little sympathy if they lagged at reveille.

My task, as the new majority leader, wasn't going to be as easy as getting Ed to give Tom Hauke and Gary Johnson better committee assignments. It became apparent that the power of the Speaker needed to be knocked down a peg or two in the view of the conservatives, something I was reluctant to help accommodate.

The Climax

Things came to a head at the end of January. The combatants' anger and mistrust had poisoned the caucus room. The yelling was not going to produce a catharsis. There would be no weeping and making up, followed by some deal that would allow the Democrats to march onto the floor united. I decided to ask Tom Hauke if he would place the motion to replace Ed. My question put Hauke in a bind: he could only say yes or no. Up until this point, no one had actually asked this question. Left unanswered, it provided some security to both sides. Had I more experience, I would have made sure a third option was available.

Hauke yelled "yes" in a voice perhaps last heard at Little Big Horn. The battle was joined. He would make the motion when we convened on Tuesday of the next week. The Speaker said that if the motion to oust him succeeded, "it would be the end of party government as we know it in Wisconsin."[2]

A committee was appointed in the caucus. It consisted of Ed and me, representing "the Crown"; Gary Johnson and the Speaker pro tem, Louise Tesmer, representing the challengers; and Jim Rooney, the caucus chair. He was expected to be neutral, a role he was well equipped for since he was androgynous in ideology and no-nonsense in approach.

I was now firmly established as an ally of Ed. Rooney shuttled between us and the other faction. This meant that I dealt with Rooney, and Ed was helpless when I made a concession. However, if a conservative got something, it meant an Ed loyalist lost something, and I would have to deliver the news. This process certainly honed my negotiating skills because I had to make people who were giving up things, like their brand-new, plum committee assignment, feel like they were doing something for a greater good. Some days altruism was as rare as a lobbyist with a sack lunch.

Ed and I would huddle in his office throughout the day. He slumped in his leather chair. I sprawled on the couch with my legs on the coffee table. In that smoky room we camped out, like officers far from battle who only hear old news and whose orders may or may not go through. Our talk was of the war, but we did not seem to be in it.

The issue was not coming down to committees, or the power of the Speaker, or even replacing Ed. Hauke and the conservative Democrats

---

[2] *Wisconsin State Journal*, January 29, 1981.

wanted Ed to know he was the problem and say it. They wanted Ed to admit that he was abrasive and arrogant and symbolic of everything wrong with the old order.

I wanted Ed to spill his guts in front of the caucus. I said, "Admit to some things; say you were wrong about some things. They want to hear you say that you are not Mr. Personality." He could not. It was not that he thought it wouldn't help, or it wasn't true. He just couldn't do it because he couldn't pull it off. Ed's reaction to public speaking ranged from nervous to terrified. The thought of standing before his colleagues in the caucus room, with the door closed and all eyes on him, like the audience in the last act expecting the soliloquy that would precede the tragic end of the flawed hero, was too much for him.

Besides, what about the true good he had done? Hadn't he busted the Finance Committee's lock on big decisions? Hadn't he reformed the budget process? Did he have to suffer fools and be criticized if he didn't say "hi" to some nincompoop he passed in the hall?

Although he couldn't confess to the caucus, in our shared foxhole things human and fine shone through. Ed was not who they said he was. He was not who I thought he was. He was the person and the talented leader the members had discerned—the sculpture not the stone. For good reason they had thought enough of him to elect him Speaker three times.

NIGHT INTRIGUES

Night was like Halloween. I would go from office to office, sometimes with Rooney, sometimes alone, trying to cut a deal with whatever gaggle from the other side I could find. The treat was something better than they had now. I was out of tricks. Like the guy on the Ed Sullivan Show who keeps the dishes spinning on top of those sticks, I just tried to keep it going so nothing would break. One night the chairman of the Finance Committee, John Norquist, and I had the sergeant-at-arms unlock the office next to Hauke's. There in the dark we tried to listen through the closed adjoining door by placing a water glass against it. We took turns pressing our ear against the base of the glass, hoping to hear what someone was holding out for, so we could know the real bottom line. This may work in the movies, but we didn't hear anything clearly. We took two beers from the refrigerator in that office and left.

Another night a thick-tongued voice on the phone summoned me to the Madison Club. At a table chosen for its prominence sat three of the Democratic conspirators from the other side and the Republican governor, Lee Sherman Dreyfus. The legislators had been drinking. The governor wanted to be there about as much as a turtle wants to be on top of a post. He was locked in by the others, who had already reached the cigar stage of male inebriation. The message to me was supposed to be that he was playing ball with them, and "they" could control reapportionment (which would have to be dealt with later in the session). Governor Dreyfus's interest in government was ephemeral, and the nitty-gritty of internal politics interested him not at all. I could see that the thought of having these good old boys as allies had already scuttled the deal. I left.

THE COUP FAILS

Often in a legislature the answer is reapportionment regardless of what the question happens to be. A deal was starting to form that would make Hauke a co-chair of a new reapportionment committee. It would be Hauke and Bill Broydrick, an ally of Ed and a member of the Tuesday Club.

The other part of the deal concerned appointments to conference committees. In the future an informal "leadership committee," which would include members of the conservative wing of the Democratic caucus, would sign off on appointments to conference committees. It was also assumed that in the next session the Speaker, whoever it was, would need to get approval of his or her regular committee assignments from this group. Finally, Gary Johnson and Tom Hauke and their followers were given better committee assignments. The package was agreed to, and Hauke announced he would not make a motion to dump the Speaker.

It took several weeks and all my energy to negotiate the deal, but the hard part was to get Ed to agree to it. He did, but only after I made sure that the committee designed to check the Speaker's power would not be written into the rule book. This was fortuitous, and showed Ed's grasp of the big picture, because during the next session I was elected Speaker, and the idea of the watchdog committee was quietly forgotten.

THE LESSONS LEARNED

The next session Ed did not seek reelection. He was going to look for a real job that paid enough so he could start to build some future security for his family, which now included a second child. Although some tested the water, none decided to get wet. I ran for Speaker without any opposition, and this would be the case in the three subsequent times I was elected Speaker.

Because of my long apprenticeship, I knew how to change the things that were wrong or unfair when I became the Speaker. And I knew how to listen. I often told the members of the caucus to think carefully about what committee assignment they asked me for because they might get it. I talked with each member long enough to discern the assignment each wanted. What my colleagues wanted was often different from what they asked for because they would take the needs of other members into account.

The conservatives were made a part of the team in this way. If someone complained or criticized the direction we were going, I would appoint them on the spot to head a group to decide a new direction. I made a deal with the minority leader: I would tell him in advance what we were going to do, and he agreed to do the same.

I eventually got to the point during my long tenure as Speaker where I would simply ask the Democrats to trust me. I might not tell them all the stops along the way, but I would get them to the desired destination. A Speaker must see the goal and not worry too much about how to get there. Unexpected things will happen along the way to the goal. But a leader who has been a student and knows the people in the institution and its history, can, if he or she lets go of some power and gives power to others, be free to lead. It is the light grip and the relaxed fluid swing that hits the ball where it is supposed to go.

Branches of State Government:
The Separation of Unequal Powers

If, on the other hand, a legislative power could be so constituted as to represent the majority without necessarily being the slave of its passions, an executive so as to retain a proper share of authority, and a judiciary so as to remain independent of the other two powers, a government would be formed which would still be democratic, without incurring hardly any risk of tyranny.[1]

Alexis De Tocqueville

The relationship between a state legislature and the governor is molded by party affiliation, division of power, and the need for legislative leaders to defend their institution against raids on its power from the governor, and vice versa. The legislature appears equal in power to the governor; after all, they both have to agree in order to change any law or spend tax money. However, the governor's veto power is the weapon in his or her arsenal that tips the balance of power in favor of the executive.

The veto power varies. The governor of North Carolina does not have the power to veto legislation. In some states a veto can be overridden with only a majority vote of both houses of the legislature. In Wisconsin a veto requires a two-thirds vote of both houses, which means that it is almost impossible to override. This type of supermajority is the norm among the states.

Sometimes there is a fight between the legislature and the executive over who has what power, and the state supreme court is asked to referee.

---

[1] Alexis De Tocqueville, *Democracy in America*, specially edited and abridged for the modern reader by Richard D. Heffner (New York: Mentor, 1956), 102.

Courts are usually dragged reluctantly into these "political" battles over turf. Yet in a system of divided government designed to check one branch from becoming too powerful, it is often only the court that can keep equilibrium in this balance of power.

Power is divided and limited because those elected to high office will exercise every bit of power they are granted and no less. And the limits on power, if they are tested and seem elastic, will be stretched and stretched some more. It is the way of those men and women who wield power in government, any government.

In this chapter I explain three different roles a legislative leader can play in interactions with the executive branch: the "loyal opposition" role, exercised when the leader is in the majority party and the governor is of the other party; the "lieutenant" role, exercised when the governor's office and the legislature are controlled by the same party; and the "defender-of-the-institution" role, exercised when the legislature's prerogatives are under assault by the executive branch.

EQUAL IN THEORY

Theoretically, the legislature and the executive branch of state government are equal. The legislature passes proposed laws and appropriates money. The governor decides whether to sign the proposals and spend the money or say "no" with a veto. Neither can change the law without the assent of the other.

No better insight can be gained into the relationship of legislatures and governors than to keep in mind that when the colonial legislatures became state legislatures after the American Revolution, the new office of governor was to be watched and held on a short leash by legislative power. The fear was that the governor would become king. After all, the king of England had appointed the colonial governors. Although legislatures could represent the colonists in many areas (and could wield significant control over taxing and spending, for example), on many important things the governor called the shots, and there was no redress.

When deciding to check the power of the executive, the colonists had in mind at least two kinds of governors: the popular governor, perhaps a war hero, who might become a people's king, and a demagogue, who might win the people's loyalty through appeals to emotion and prejudice. Therefore, the governor's tenure was made short and limited to one or two terms. Also the power of the office was dispersed by placing certain executive functions in other statewide constitutional offices, such as treasurer.

There is a genius to the American system of divided power. It lies in the legislatures that were created. It is no trick to invent a government and devise a strong executive. The pharaoh, the king, the dictator, the emperor are the norm of history. The trick of democracy is to devise a strong legislature that can survive transfers of power and shifts of party control.

Late in 1990 I conducted a workshop for the first postcommunist parliament of the newly free and independent country of Hungary. There had been elected parliaments before in this country's long history, interspersed between monarchs and emperors, but their shelf life had not been long. The national gallery housed in a castle on the hill in Budapest, high above the Danube, is full of paintings of men on white horses who took or were given near absolute power when things went wrong in Hungary. This is a tendency in all forms of government. If there had not been obstacles in the way, like Congress and the state legislatures, it might have happened in the American democracy.

In the legislative institution in a functioning democracy, two things are necessary for longevity. First, the party in the majority must remember and be reminded that its situation is temporary, and the party out of power must believe that its situation is temporary as well. In this way both the "ins" and the "outs" have a reason to act as stewards of the institution. Second, the denizens of the legislature, the mere mortals elected to visit the joint for brief periods, must be handcuffed by the Constitution, law, and rule to prevent them from giving away their power, either through lack of use, or by outright grant, to the president or the governor. And the institution must have another legal wall around it so the president or the governor does not simply take power when its ownership is debatable.

LEGISLATIVE LEADERSHIP

The office of Speaker is often called the second most powerful post in state government after the governorship. Indeed, the Speaker can arrange things so his or her office becomes a funnel with a spigot on the end. All things—appointments of committee chairs, referral of bills, interpretation of the rules, and so on—flow to the Speaker's office; when or if they flow out is determined when and if the spigot is turned. Like the Speaker, the leader of the state Senate has this power, but the spigot is leakier because there are more hands on the handle. In state Senates, power is usually divided among several leaders.

Party affiliation largely determines the role of the legislative leader. If the governor is of the same party, the Speaker becomes the governor's lieutenant in addition to his or her role as a legislative leader. If the governor is of the other party, the Speaker becomes the leader of the loyal opposition, and a legislative leader, *and* a lieutenant of the governor. In this latter role the Speaker may be a surly subordinate, and the relationship is tentative and suspicious. The chain of command works as you may expect, about as well as a Turkish general trying to give orders to a Greek colonel. Nevertheless, the governor, not the legislative leader, sets the agenda. In short, party is the most important factor determining the relationship between the legislative and executive branches.

The minority leader becomes a lieutenant to a governor of his or her party. And this is a more subservient brand of junior officer because power for the minority party in the legislature comes from sticking with the leader of its party in the state, the governor, and not tilting at some windmill that may seem inviting but is down a side road. If the governor is of the other party, the minority leader heads the loyal opposition. The minority leader must fight for marginal influence by concentrating on the differences between the two parties that are stark enough and controversial enough that compromise with the minority is in the political self-interest of the majority.

The working relationship between the two houses of a legislature also depends on the party of the governor and whether the majority party in both houses is the same or divided. However, other things come into play that are more important. One of the basic jobs of the leaders of the two houses is to reconcile the differences between the two houses on important and controversial legislation. It follows then that it is their job to move their house closer to the position of the other house. This is delicate work, and the negotiating process works best when the leaders are friends, regardless of party. It doesn't work well at all when the leaders are not friends or, worse, if they are rivals. If one leader disparages the leader of the other house, it is in very bad taste. This is the worst sin and a sure sign the leaders have yet to learn their craft.

Senate Majority Leader Tim Cullen was my counterpart for several years during my Speakership. We were friends, and our relationship was congenial. After some maneuver of Tim's would go well in the Senate, which it usually did, he would say with a bright smile, "I'm just an Irish politician." He was a master at massaging the egos in the place, which grew every time the fertilizer of being called "senator" was applied.

We were in so many seemingly hopeless situations together that after a few years we actually formulated a few informal rules. The first was, no surprises. He would let me know what to expect from the Senate, and I would do my best to predict things in the Assembly. Rule 2 was to pretend (especially in public) that it wasn't a surprise if Rule 1 failed. If the Senate did the opposite of what Tim had told me would happen, and a reporter got to me first, I might say, "Tim and I talked and this looked like it might happen." Then I would call him and ask him what went wrong. Rule 3 was to defend each other in our respective caucuses. When the two houses are at odds, it is easy to blame the leader of the other house when the differences seem irreconcilable. Many a time in my caucus did I refute someone's claim regarding Tim's lineage, and he did the same in his caucus for me. Finally, when we wanted to state the position of our party, or make some other grandiose claim, we would do it when the legislature was out of session, lest a vote on the floor prove the opposite was true.

In my dealings with Assembly Minority Leader Tommy Thompson, the rule "no surprises" meant that we would try and tell each other what our plans were in advance. For example, I might tell him, "I will offer the amendment we [the Democrats] really care about after amendment seven." Or, "I don't have the votes, so we are going to hide in the caucus room. When you get tired of waiting, about five o'clock, send in a message, and I will say we might as well adjourn until tomorrow. Deal? OK."

The relationship between the leaders of the two houses, and the relationship between the majority and minority party leaders, is important because their roles as agents or partisan opponents of the governor are secondary to their roles as representatives of the legislature. In a system of divided power, their first loyalty must be to the institution in which they serve.

LEADER OF THE OPPOSITION

Republican Lee Sherman Dreyfus was elected governor because under the Democratic incumbent governor the state accumulated an embarrassing $1 billion surplus that was growing. Wages were chasing the double-digit inflation of the Carter years, pushing more people into the higher state income tax rates, and the system simply took in more money than could be spent. Dreyfus, the chancellor of the University of Wisconsin at Stevens Point, had perhaps the best political idea in the history of campaigns when he proposed to "withhold the withholding"—not collect future taxes until the surplus was gone by stopping the withholding of state income taxes.

The Democrats in the legislature (the majority party) were terrified. This new populist Republican governor was not a definable politician, he was as well liked as bratwurst, and he had the press baffled. He did not issue written press releases, and he talked so fast that the capital reporters had to give up their pencils and notebooks and use tape recorders instead so that they could listen to him later, at a slower speed, in order to get their quotes right.

How, if you are the leadership of the Democratic Party in the Assembly and the state Senate, can you oppose the governor of the other party if his proposal is to lower taxes, and fast? A huge surplus is impossible to justify in politics. The Democratic leaders in the house and the Senate actually talked a lot about what possible alternative could exist. Sen. Paul Offner, a member of the Finance Committee, said at one meeting: "There must be a Democratic way to lower taxes." We all felt we had to put some stamp on the tax cut to avoid being run over on upcoming issues, like the state budget, by the popular governor. And we had to show some party cohesion. What did we do? We lowered taxes by withholding the withholding, but we lowered them more than the governor had proposed.

If the Republicans were for tax cuts, the Democrats were for even deeper tax cuts. Ed Jackamonis, the Speaker, actually said in our caucus, "We will lower taxes so much there will be a deficit when Dreyfus runs for reelection." This was a lot of barroom talk since the election was three years away.

The room was packed at the ceremony when the tax cut bill was signed, and the governor handed us all one of his trademark red pens with red ink. Here was a piece of legislation with more authors than a library. Incredibly, the nation's and the state's economy fell apart as fast as we gave away the $1 billion surplus. During the last two years of Dreyfus's term, there loomed on the near horizon a potential deficit of at least $1 billion. The red pens with red ink took on an ironic new meaning. It was at the start of this session that I was elected the majority leader. The Democrats were still in control, having survived being on the same ballot as Ronald Reagan and his landslide of votes, but we were badly split on ideological lines—the conservatives had tried to dump Speaker Jackamonis. What was worse, the gorilla of reapportionment had to be danced with before the session ended. It was getting to be that time in the decade.

To deal with the deficit, Governor Dreyfus proposed an increase in the sales tax from 4 to 5 percent. So here I was, part of a team of leaders being asked to raise taxes at the behest of a governor of the other party. There was no question among us that this was our responsibility. The debate was over whether to substitute an income tax hike for the governor's proposed sales tax hike. Democrats were against the sales tax. It was regressive and presumably hated by the people. It was gospel among state Democrats that we had gained our success and turned Wisconsin into a two-party state because the Republicans had embraced the state's first general sales tax a decade earlier.

John Norquist, the Finance Committee chair, and I proposed as a substitute for the sales tax increase a temporary income tax hike of 8 percent. The proposal made the headlines in the morning papers. By the afternoon this trial balloon had crashed and burned like the Hindenburg. It turned out that the sales tax had lost its stigma. In the end we led our troops to vote for the sales tax, which was to be "temporary," and we mandated under the law a 4 percent tax after two years. We demanded that at least some Republican leaders vote for it, and the day we got the needed votes, Dreyfus, in operatic timing, announced he would not run again. Great! Now we were leaders, of both the majority and the minority, raising taxes for a lame duck governor.

GUBERNATORIAL LEADERSHIP

I grew to like Lee Dreyfus. The people he brought to state government were first-class human beings with a regard for the mystery of democracy and the attitude that they were stewards of power for just a short time. The people of the state were well served. He was my favorite dinner companion, and I can give no higher compliment to a Republican. Our friendship was cemented during a trade mission to the People's Republic of China in 1981. There hadn't been too many official visitors since President Richard Nixon and Secretary of State Henry Kissinger visited in the early 1970s after relations between the United States and the People's Republic of China were restored. Governor Dreyfus slept (until quite late in the morning) in the former palace where the government had housed Nixon, and I slept down the hall in the Kissinger bed, which was lumpy. I doubt if we sold a kernel of corn, but it was a great trip and because of it we could work together later when the state's economy fell apart.

Governor Dreyfus had the philosophy that the "governor proposes and the legislature disposes." The legislative leaders trotted out a lot of alternatives, but in the end, after chewing on it a while and modifying it a bit, we usually passed what the governor had initiated. Because of the deep recession, there were few viable alternatives. The governor had the policymaking role. As leaders of the loyal opposition in the legislature, we offered substitute ideas that fit our party's philosophy better, but our role was not to propose and pass an alternate path for the state, especially in a time of financial crisis. The job of the leaders changed, but not too much, with the next governor, Democrat Tony Earl.

LIEUTENANT TO THE GOVERNOR

Much of politics is about garnish rather than meat and potatoes. Big issues, like poverty, are there but the debate and the proposals offered are marginal in their scope. The Democrats may want parsley and the Republicans may want a slice of lemon. The difference is not substantial and deals with appearance. Political success, which has very low standards of judgment, has more to do with how the waiter—the politician—serves the meal than with the quality of the food.

Democratic governor Tony Earl liked to serve liver without garnish because it was good for the body politic. He felt if the dish was nourishing, the presentation didn't matter. He often said that "good policy makes good politics," and he was wrong. There may be an ounce of truth somewhere in this bromide, but Tony Earl never found it. Tony was a successful governor (in terms of enacting progressive legislation), but he was not good at presenting, or explaining, to the public these controversial policy changes. Because of this my stint as his lieutenant was a tough posting.

Tony came into office promising a tax increase. The recession still raged, and another deficit of more than $1 billion in the state budget was forecast largely because of the scheduled automatic reduction in the sales tax. This deficit, 20 percent of state expenditures, could be closed only by taxes. The temporary sales tax proposed by Dreyfus and passed in the last session had to be made permanent at 5 percent. The Democrats, the majority party in both houses, had to pass a budget. The governor had proposed a set of taxes, and, believe me, when it comes to raising taxes every legislature has a yellow stripe right down the center aisle dividing the parties. Better that the other side propose the increase.

Tony balanced the books by making the sales tax permanent and by enacting an income tax surcharge, which he had promised to do. As a result, he gained the moniker of "Tony the Taxer." The Democrats were interested in a nap after this exercise, but the governor had other things in mind. He proposed several controversial initiatives, such as pay equity for male and female state employees and changing Wisconsin to a marital property state. Despite working hard on sensible things to help the state's economy, he was blamed for a "bad business climate." This is a charge a liberal Democrat finds hard to answer, and Tony fell into the trap of using facts to justify his initiatives.

The Democrats loved Tony, the former majority leader in the Assembly. He liked beer, pinochle, politics, and politicians. The Republicans liked Tony for the same reasons. He was a gentleman who respected the legislature as an institution. His friends were those from both parties that he had served with in the Assembly.

Tony and I were friends (I had supported him in the primary), and I wanted him to be successful and that simply meant that I worked hard to get his program passed. My deal with Tony was straightforward. I would try to push his agenda and keep the good-sounding but bad public-policy bills off his desk so he wouldn't have to take the rap for vetoing them. In return he had to bend a little on his absolutism on good government and engage in some good politics by giving the Democrats who were voting for his stuff some bacon to bring back to their districts. My role, in addition to playing the loyal lieutenant, was to broker the needs of the Democrats in the Assembly with the governor. If they were going to vote for his nourishing but politically hard-to-digest hunks of liver, they wanted him to swallow their pork.

The Democrats seemed to be continually voting for unpopular but theoretically good measures that they had a tough time explaining. And I kept asking them to explain. The problem was that in return Tony would often balk at helping Democrats because what they wanted was, in his opinion, bad public policy. The epitome of this yin without the yang was Lowell Jackson, the governor's transportation secretary. Lowell had been the head of the Department of Transportation under Governor Dreyfus and ran for governor when Dreyfus quit. Tony and Lowell hit it off while debating each other in the primary, which came about because the front-runners of the two parties would not be on the same platform with these two long shots. Lowell didn't make it through the Republican primary, but Tony, the Democrat, made it all the way to the governor's office and hired his new-found friend Lowell, the Republican, to again be in charge of highways. Bringing his new friend home to the Democrats may have sounded good at the time. However, like meeting and marrying someone from a different culture after a twenty-four-hour romance on a South Pacific island, you learn things will not be as idyllic on the mainland.

Lowell, despite his training as an engineer and his previous love affair with cement, did not want to build highways, especially in Democratic districts, and particularly not in mine! Denying a legislator cement or asphalt is like taking the saddle away from a cowboy. Irritation is the result.

When push came to shove, I had to give up the governor and pay attention to the needs of my caucus, the ones who elected me as their Speaker. Tensions came to a head when Tony, in a move that was personally embarrassing for me, vetoed a needed and promised upgrade of an unsafe highway in my district. I had to part with him to show the legislative Democrats that there was no question: I was their agent, and I was on their side. I knew what was stuck in their craw and exactly what they were saying to themselves about the governor: "We carried your water until our arms were so long we could tie our shoes without bending over, and the thanks we get is a veto recommended by a Republican and a lecture about good government."

The Democratic leaders wore two hats during Governor Earl's tenure. We were his lieutenants as members of the same party, working to push his policies (as well as make them more acceptable to the Democrats). Then we had to don the hat of the defender when Governor Earl tried to expand his power at the expense of the legislature. This happened when he abused his veto power. He put Tim Cullen and me in the position of standing up for the institution or standing by the governor. It was an easy choice.

THE VETO

The American system of divided government is not based on the idea that the legislature and the governor, or Congress and the president, are separate entities but still partners, like married couples. A better analogy is partners in a business with a checking account that requires two signatures on a check. The legislature can write in an amount, taking note of the balance, and sign its name on one line. But no cash goes out of the account, and no law goes on the books, unless the other partner, the governor, signs his or her name. The governor is the senior partner because if he or she doesn't sign nothing happens. The veto is the act of not signing a bill passed by the legislature.

An *item veto* offers a governor the option of not signing a minor part of a bill and letting the rest of it become law. In the fifty states the effect of this veto power varies. Sometimes a separate new law included as part of a larger bill (a budget bill, for example) can be vetoed out of that bill. In other states the veto power is granted to the governor for the express purpose of reducing expenditures, which is why it is often called a *line item veto.* Most governors, through the use of their partial veto power, can reduce an amount of money appropriated by the legislature. Governors in this way can select the new spending they wish to oppose. Or perhaps because governors look farther ahead than legislatures usually do, the veto is employed as a way to avoid committing to future obligations and thus chart a more prudent fiscal course.

Indeed, the governor of Wisconsin can exercise the partial veto only on bills that spend money. (The bill can be on any subject.) Use of the partial veto has usually been restricted to the state budget bill. Unlike all other states, the Wisconsin constitution uses the phrase "veto in part" rather than "item veto." The last five governors have expanded the meaning of a "part" of a bill. Gov. Tony Earl tried a cute maneuver that absolutely had to be challenged by the legislative leaders of his own party.

If "part" really meant "part," then a part of a number or parts of a sentence could be vetoed to make a new number or a new sentence, hence a new law. And this is what Tony tried. He reduced a paragraph consisting of five sentences (121 words) to one sentence of 22 words, some of which were made up of the single letters left over from the parts of other words he had vetoed! The "law" that would have resulted from this pick-a-letter process had an intent that was the opposite of that passed by the legislature. The Democratic leaders huddled and demanded that every last Democrat vote to override this veto. And they did. All of the Democrats in both houses voted to override as did all the Republicans.

Unfortunately, the lesson learned by one attentive member of the Assembly, Minority Leader Thompson, who would soon be governor, was that if the governor had the votes to sustain his vetoes he would have the power, through the pick-a-letter veto, to get away with murder. Tommy Thompson defeated Tony Earl, and for four years, until I ran against him for governor, I was Governor Thompson's loyal opposition. He used the pick-a-letter veto on his first budget bill with a vengeance. The resulting fight over what the phrase "veto in part" meant ended up before the state supreme court.

CHALLENGING THE GOVERNOR'S VETO

It was only a matter of time before the scope of the governor's veto was again addressed by the court. But it took a while. Democratic governor Pat Lucey had tried to reduce a bonding program from $25 million to $5 million by crossing out the "2." He let the program go at the higher figure when the state attorney general said the legality of the bonds might come into question if this veto was taken to the court. Governor Earl's pick-a-letter veto was overridden, so again the veto was not challenged in this instance. However, in two previous cases brought by the legislature, the court had built upon a 1935 decision that construed the "veto in part" to be a power greater than that of an "item veto." [2] The court had laid down the principle that the governor's power to legislate was coextensive with the legislature's.

At the age of twenty-five, Tommy Thompson was elected in 1966 to the Assembly from a rural and very Republican district in the center of the state. Conservative, talented, and eager, he was a favorite of the extremely conservative leadership in the Assembly and was appointed to serve on the prestigious Finance Committee his first term—a real plum for a freshman. In 1970 the Democrats won control of the Assembly, which marked the final passing of Wisconsin from a one-party state (Republican) to a competitive two-party state.

Tommy became the minority leader in the Assembly in 1981, the start of the sales tax half of the Dreyfus term, and the two of us had a friendly working relationship throughout those two years and the four years of Tony Earl's term.

Tommy (the name fit his boyish looks) was a frustrated minority leader. Under Dreyfus he had to push the sales tax increase, and then he had victory snatched from him on several bills where it appeared he had the votes to defeat a liberal policy pushed by Governor Earl. He seemed to be against everything, thus earning him the appellation "Dr. No." He was

---

[2] *State ex. rel. Wisconsin Telephone Co.* v. *Henry*, 218 Wis. (1935).

not the early favorite in his race against Earl, but Earl's successes in the legislature were not popular with the voters. Tony's controversial record, and the times, seemed to dictate that the state swing back to a more conservative course, the historical norm.

But Tommy Thompson, the new governor, was still stuck with a Democratic legislature that was battle-hardened from the Dreyfus siege and the trench warfare for Earl. It had withstood the conservative offensive of the two Reagan campaigns and was feeling immortal. So perhaps it is not surprising that this governor gave into temptation and used his veto power to, in effect, retype the state budget bill. He made almost 300 partial vetoes, taking a part of a word here and a part of a sentence there to reshape the bill as he felt it should read. When he was finished there remained scant evidence of the version passed by the legislature. If this act of massive rewriting was allowed to stand, a dangerous precedent would be set, and this governor and future governors would have a new power. Therefore, the legislature decided to challenge the way the governor had exercised his veto power. We went back to the state supreme court to try our luck for a third time in less than two decades.

The governor's creative use of the veto power enabled him to write a new law that went into effect if only one-third plus one of the members of one house of the legislature voted to sustain the veto. Two-thirds of both houses had to say no to override the veto. The idea that the assent of both houses of the legislature and the governor is required to enact a law, which is one of the purposes of our system of divided government, was thrown out the window if the governor could write a new law simply by playing a one-man game of Scrabble.

I really wanted to go to court. How else could this thing be undone? There was no way to override the vetoes, since we needed Republicans to help, and even if we did override, this would send the wrong message: it would seem like the legislature endorsed the idea that the governor had the power and only disagreed on how it was used in a particular instance. It was technically possible, but not realistic or desirable, to separate in every bill the money from the policy and pass two bills, one with the "appropriation" and a companion with the policy. Long gone were the days when spending was restricted to the state budget bill. Almost every bill of any consequence contained an appropriation for funding. Finally, we could find no way to amend the constitution (redefine the word "part") to put the scales back in balance.

Our attorney, Brady Williamson, said it was a tough case, but there was a reasonable chance of winning if one had faith that the law the court had made was corrigible. This court had already stated its views on the veto power, and the chief justice himself, Nathan Heffernan, had written the most recent opinion on the issue. But surely this new thing, where (as we pointed out in our brief) the "governor alone" writes "new law" from parts of words and sentences, will be recognized by the same court as going too far. So we thought.

Unfortunately, the chief justice held to his previous line of reasoning, regardless of where this governor led him to follow it. He declared that "the governor has the authority to veto sections, subsections, paragraphs, sentences, words, parts of words, letters and digits included in an appropriation bill as long as what remains is a complete and workable law." He added that the resulting new law must be "germane"—on the same subject as the vetoed parts.[3]

It was a four to three decision, and the dissent was written by Justice William Bablitch, a Democrat and the former majority leader in the state Senate. "Ordinarily, for a bill to become a law it must pass both houses of the legislature with a majority vote in each, and then be approved by the governor," he wrote. To give an example of the governor's new power, Justice Bablitch used language inserted by the legislature in the budget bill to increase the penalty for murder.

> 940.03 Felony murder. Whoever causes the death of another human being while committing or attempting to commit another crime [such as armed robbery] may be imprisoned for not more than 20 years in excess of the maximum period of imprisonment provided by law for that crime or attempt.

Justice Bablitch pointed out that if the governor left the sentence intact up to the words "may be" and then crossed out all but the letters underlined, the new words would enact the death penalty (something that has never reached first base in this century in the Wisconsin legislature). And since the letters were stricken from words dealing with the penalty for murder, the veto would meet the germaneness test.

The chief justice, in a written aside at the end of the decision, told Bablitch that the legislature shouldn't add language dealing with criminal law to the budget bill and if it does, to "assume it will be insulated from the governor's partial veto power, is little short of fatuous." It is a good thing a question on the prohibition in the Wisconsin constitution on granting hereditary titles wasn't before the chief justice because he might have declared a monarchy on the spot.

The legislature could not easily defend itself against the governor's new lawmaking power. And, of course, careful defensive action did nothing to reduce or change the power. Furthermore, a future legislature, interested in complicity with the governor, could simply pass bills and then

---

[3] *State ex. rel. Wisconsin Senate* v. *Thompson,* 144 Wis. 2d. (1988).

encourage the governor to indulge, like a hungry kid with a spoon sitting down to an inviting bowl of alphabet soup.

There was press criticism and a moderate public outcry following the governor's vetoes and Chief Justice Heffernan's decision to uphold them. The Democrats in the legislature were able, but just barely, to move a constitutional change through the legislature and onto the ballot that eliminated the power to cross out letters to form new words. It was adopted by the voters, but the governor's unilateral ability to make new law by crossing out words to make new sentences remains.

The idea of separating the executive budget into several bills in order to limit the governor's veto opportunities did not interest the members of the legislature. This was true even though Governor Thompson had submitted separate bills, and I had urged the Democrats to go along with this because it was in the legislature's self-interest.

The reality was that the members of the legislature did not see themselves, when added together, to be the institution of the legislature. The members, especially the Finance Committee members, did not want to try to rectify the institution's new subservient status, if it meant that they gave up their individual power to add their policy items to the budget bill. The members would have to become individually weaker in order for the legislature to regain some strength vis-à-vis the governor, and they wanted nothing to do with this equation.

Alas, the Wisconsin legislature is now accustomed to this junior status. It is like a small and weak country aligned with a large power. It is independent but has little say.

THE LESSONS

I did not realize that if I, as the Speaker, took the legislature's ball and bat to the state supreme court, I would be going to a place where they were not playing baseball. The role of the legislative leader is to look out for his or her institution, whether the members care or not. Only in theory, not in practice, is the legislature coequal with the governor. But the leaders must proceed as if equality is the case.

Political power should be checked by law and process and by dividing it up because mere mortals, when elected to high office, will not exercise self-restraint. Governor Earl took power from the legislature because it was there to be taken. A legislature would do the same if it had the opportunity.

The power to legislate by veto now enjoyed by Wisconsin governors is only really limited by self-restraint. Chief Justice Heffernan and the court majority, believing in the infallibility of their own reasoning, walked the constitution down a primrose path to a dead end, and they have left no map showing how to get back to a system of checks and balances.

The veto power of a president or governor can determine whether a legislature, and thus the democracy, will be vibrant or weak. I oppose giving the president of the United States the item veto.

The veto power found in most state constitutions defines the governor as the senior partner in the business of government in the states. However, a less obvious power, the governor's power to propose budgets, is what really gives a governor the tiller when it comes to setting the course of policy.

The power of a governor to propose is what allows him or her to set the agenda in a state. In all but two states the governor proposes the state budget. The budget bill sets the taxing and spending policy of the state for a one- or two-year period, and it must pass. This bill is what the legislature debates. It sets the legislature's agenda.

When Wisconsin enjoyed a $1 billion surplus, it was Governor Dreyfus who proposed that the money be returned in the form of a tax decrease, rather than being spent, saved, or used to retire debt. The legislature did not have a real alternative to this basic policy choice of the governor. In fact, as is the case in every state legislature save two, the budget process makes the executive budget the document to work from. It can be amended, but rarely will it be replaced by an alternative generated in the legislature. It is like being presented with a ship in a bottle. You can alter the ship, perhaps paint it a different color, or even make it look like a freighter instead of a frigate, but it has to remain a ship, and it can't be taken out of the bottle.

Wisconsin was presented with a $1 billion deficit when Governor Tony Earl took office, and it was the governor who presented the outline of the plan to close this revenue gap. The legislature did some major tinkering (reformed the income tax system), but the governor's proposed formula was eventually passed.

Of course, legislatures routinely deny governors things they want. All governors have some wish list of campaign promises, or bones they need to throw their allies in interest groups, but these things are different. The legislature is coequal when it comes to saying no. However, the state budget bill or a solution to the crisis of the moment must pass, and it is here, on the most important issues, where the governor calls the shots. When you brush aside the ifs and buts, what remains is an unequal relationship between legislatures and governors. The governor can propose, say yes and say no. The legislature can only count on the power to say no.

The Abortion Issue:
Conflict Without Resolution

The legislative process is designed to produce compromise. Its many features—decision making by committee, amendments, the requirement that a proposed law pass both houses in identical form, the veto power of the governor (in effect telling the legislature to try again) are like machines on an assembly line, operating together to manufacture a consensus. The issue of abortion does not lend itself to this process, however. The two politically powerful pressure groups—the "pro-choice" side and the "pro-life" side—do not want compromise, and on this issue they control the agenda. This is the case in almost all state legislatures.

STRATEGIC CONSIDERATIONS

During every session there was one strategically important anti-abortion bill before the legislature. The pro-choice side, which included the Democratic leadership, tried to keep the bill bottled up in committee, and the pro-life side, through political pressure on the Republicans and conservative Democrats, tried to pull it out so the whole Assembly could vote on it on the floor of the chamber. If the pro-life people could get the bill to the floor for a vote, they would win. To accomplish this end, they needed to gain supporters from the pivotal middle group of legislators, usually moderates of both parties from marginal districts.

In these districts the pro-life foot soldiers were strategically placed and well organized. This explains why the pro-life side had a majority in the legislature, even though poll after poll showed that the people of Wisconsin did not support anything that would, in effect, make abortion illegal. Any real restrictions on a woman's right to an abortion that might pass the legislature had already been ruled unconstitutional in 1973 by the

U.S. Supreme Court in *Roe* v. *Wade.* The pro-life side's strategy was to bring a new state law to the Court containing some legal nuance that would present an opportunity to overturn *Roe.*

The politics of abortion in the Wisconsin legislature was trench warfare. I was in the pro-choice trench, and the goal was not to give an inch. As the Speaker, my basic job was to forge compromise, to move things along, to make the place work. But on abortion bills, it was understood that I was going to stack the deck in the Health and Human Resources Committee in favor of the pro-choice position and pull a roadblock out of my bag of parliamentary tricks when the pro-life troops started to gain ground. The expectation was that I would delay any bill from getting to the state Senate until there was too little time in the session to act on it.

Indeed, this is exactly what I did session after session. My colleagues came to recognize my "retreat to Moscow" strategy: give ground slowly, fighting all the way; extend the enemy's supply lines, secure in the knowledge that winter (the end of the session) was coming.

I knew my Democratic colleagues in the Assembly didn't want to vote on any abortion bill unless it represented a compromise that was acceptable to both sides. Normally, a study or a special committee would be the answer. A study was something to point to when justifying inaction, and it was a good bet that the process would moderate demands and produce something a member could safely support. But on this issue we were not going to produce the consensus that had eluded wiser beings throughout history. Furthermore, we were not in charge.

The pro-life side basically called the shots, and it opposed any attempt to achieve a compromise. In fact, both sides felt that compromise was a step toward defeat. The pro-life side feared compromise would be a truce; if they agreed to the armistice, they might be unable to make progress for sessions to come. The pro-choice advocates viewed compromise as appeasement. They felt that if they gave any ground, it would be a sign of weakness and would only provoke more demands.

LEGISLATIVE CONCERNS

When it came to the issue of abortion, the members of the legislature were not the generals. We were the soldiers in the line of fire. Regardless of how you voted, you were going to make a slew of single-issue voters mad. If you even said kind words about compromise, you became suspect by your own side—a potential traitor.

The legislators who felt strongly about the issue, and who wouldn't get in trouble back home if they were in the newspapers clearly stating their position on abortion, were the leaders. The legislators who had to keep their heads down because they were elected by a narrow margin, and the ones who feared a primary if one side or the other said they voted wrong, wanted something to happen but not something that would be worse than if nothing happened. This pivotal middle group, usually conservative Democrats and moderate Republicans, set the pace of change on most controversial issues. On abortion bills, however, this group couldn't win. They were mostly pro-life but seeking compromise was their nature. That is what moderates do and tend to bring about. But moving toward compromise on the issue of abortion brought them nothing but grief, especially from the major anti-abortion group, the Wisconsin Citizens Concerned for Life (WCCL).

The WCCL knew how to put pressure on these moderate legislators. In addition to the phone calls and letters to their constituents, the group might cause their indecision on the abortion issue to be mentioned in the church bulletins in their districts. Always in the minds of these vulnerable legislators was the ultimate deterrent: votes for their opponent, perhaps even a primary opponent. Like a water witch, the WCCL could find the right legislator to tap. The ones who could be pushed soon discovered Barbara Lyons, the effective WCCL lobbyist, hanging on them like a lead cape. Thus, on abortion, the most controversial of issues, moderate legislators were in a bind: publicly they urged action but privately they pleaded with me, their Speaker, to allow something to be voted on that looked like movement but really did not change the status quo. For example, as a result of this need to "do something," a bill placing some new administrative burden on doctors who performed abortions might be passed. This diverted attention from the main fight only for a short while, however.

The groups on the pro-choice side were most influential in areas represented by liberal Democrats or Republicans from the socially liberal suburbs, and these legislators were usually sure pro-choice votes anyway. Pro-choice voters who could exert pressure in legislative districts where it mattered were hard to organize. What was the pro-life threat when the Supreme Court has already spoken in *Roe?*

COUNTING VOTES

I had been involved in the abortion wars from the beginning of my legislative career. In my first session I was appointed the vice chair of the Health and Human Resources Committee in the Assembly, the committee with jurisdiction over abortion-related legislation. The issue at the time was ending funding for abortions under the state's Medicaid program, the health insurance available for women on welfare.

I was on that committee until I was elected majority leader two sessions later. For four years I sat through every public hearing on abortion legislation, helped form the bills that went to the floor, answered a ton of mail, and explained my position over and over again. On the Sunday of the week a hearing or vote was scheduled, the WCCL routinely placed leaflets about me under the windshield wipers of the cars parked at the Catholic churches in my district.

When the bill restricting Medicaid funding was debated, all the modifying amendments were rejected, and the extreme version was sent to the Democratic governor. He vetoed it, and we promptly took up a similar bill. After a gut-wrenching debate that lasted all night, an amendment was added that left it possible for the state to pay for an abortion when the mother, in the opinion of two doctors, would be permanently and severely physically disabled if the pregnancy was bought to term. This amendment represented a small victory for the pro-choice side. The governor signed the bill.

By the time I was elected Speaker, I could predict with uncanny accuracy the vote count on most important issues, including abortion. It had become second nature to me. I would see the sequence of events and maneuvers that were likely to precede the vote on the floor, calculate their impact, and know the outcome.

PARTISAN CONFLICT

The conventional wisdom in the legislature was that abortion was the one issue that was above party. Each legislator was to be allowed to vote his or her conscience. The leadership was to be benign, only asking that party members go along with it on scheduling decisions and procedural motions. This way business would be conducted in an orderly fashion, and there would be a cushion of time so the members could raise a wet finger and see which way the political winds were blowing in their districts.

In reality, however, "party" played a dominant role in the maneuvering on abortion. First, the procedural votes were often the real votes. It was the vote to pull an abortion bill out of committee that most often would be used as "your" vote on abortion in the next election. The WCCL literature would claim that your vote against scheduling the bill was a pro-abortion vote.

However, if you were a Democrat, a member of the party in the majority, you dared not vote to pull a bill, any bill. It was the clearest of the unwritten rules and there were consequences if you broke this rule. There was the real possibility the Speaker would remove you from a choice committee, and the memory among all the members of your treason would stay for your whole legislative career, like a scarlet letter only they could see.

Pulling a bill prematurely out of a committee in a legislature is an act of mutiny against the committee's chair. If one committee chair is stripped of authority to decide when to release a bill from committee, all committee chairs are open to this threat, and the Speaker and the floor leader have lost the ability to move or not move legislation in a way that addresses the public agenda but does not scuttle the party's principles in the process.

So the stakes were high. Vote to pull a bill and suffer the institutional consequences. Or vote not to pull a bill and, in the case of abortion, suffer the wrath of a powerful single-issue group that was well organized in your district.

The Republican leadership always managed to field a solid block in favor of pulling an abortion bill because it would cause holy hell to break out in the Democratic caucus and cause trouble back home for the most vulnerable Democrats. Even those Republicans who were pro-choice could be counted on to vote to pull.

The debate over abortion bills centered on the power of the majority party to keep them in committee until late in the session. A whole series of rule changes were adopted over several sessions to make the vote on pulling any bill more fail-safe, just to manage the abortion bills. The original rule was that a majority vote could pull a bill from committee to the floor of the Assembly if the bill had been in committee at least three weeks. This rule was changed a bit each session. In the end a successful motion to pull a bill moved it only to the Rules Committee for scheduling on the legislative calendar, not to the floor for a vote. The requirement that all bills in the Rules Committee be scheduled within three weeks was eliminated, and there evolved an understanding that abortion bills would not be offered as budget amendments.

THE COMMITTEE ARENA

The sanctity of not pulling bills from committee was at the heart of majority party control. The argument was that once this happened the committee system would be compromised, and the committee chair would no longer be a power to be reckoned with when it came to shaping a bill or forcing compromise. If a controversial bill was to be yanked out of a committee every time the lemming instinct clicked on in the Assembly, control would be lost and the basic power of the majority would be gone. We had the gun but the weapon would be meaningless if the other side saw us shoot one another—even once.

As the Speaker it was my job to explain over and over again that "we" did not pull bills from committees. Stating the obvious was important because experience had taught me that most of the psychological underpinnings of majority rule had to be demonstrated to the members or their learned behavior would be lost. To make sure the old dog remembers the old tricks, it has to be thrown a stick to fetch every now and again.

Although the Speaker had near dictatorial power, I learned it was wisest not to use it. However, flaunting a reminder of power, like a general using his sword as a pointer, did wonders. In a caucus during a fight on whether to pull a bill, usually the abortion bill, I might point to a committee chairman suspected to be wavering in his resolve and ask, "What does the soon-to-be-former chairman think of this maneuver?" Along with nervous laughter, this question brought some straightening of backbones among those who might think of straying.

For the newer members who might be witnessing the play for the first time, I would say to them in private: "Look, if you don't have the guts to vote with the committee on this one, it's damned unlikely that you have the guts to be a chair of any committee next session. How can I help you or name you a committee chair if you pull this stunt? The caucus would skin me if I promoted you after this. This isn't a hard vote. Why did you bust your ass to get here? So you could vote with the Republicans?"

THE UNWRITTEN RULES

The unwritten rule in the Democratic caucus that bills weren't pulled had a long history and centered around abortion bills. The rule was that if this issue needed to be dealt with, the "when" and "how" would be a "family" decision made by the majority party, not by a few Democrats voting with the Republicans. And this had to be relearned once a session.

In my second session in the Assembly we came to that predictable juncture when Rep. Joanne Duren, a Democrat from a conservative rural district, would rise to make a motion to pull the abortion bill out of committee. I had thought through a plan, and as Joanne stood waiting to be recognized, as she often did, I jumped up. I knew the Speaker, Ed Jackamonis, would call on me first because he was getting all of the housekeeping motions out of the way before proceeding to the pain of the looming debate.

Joanne was very sincere about her opposition to abortion. Abortion was wrong in her view, and it would be wrong for her not to use her position in the legislature to do something about it. However, few were sympathetic to what she wanted to force them to do: take up a resolution calling for a constitutional convention to rewrite the U.S. Constitution to outlaw abortion. For most members this was pretty farfetched, and they were irritated because this was also the WCCL's roll-call vote on abortion, and they were going to be forced to take a stand by Joanne.

The irritation was understandable. They were being told by the WCCL that they were pro-abortion unless they went along with a scheme that could reopen a discussion of every aspect of the Constitution of the United States. The plan was to have the required number of state legislatures call for a constitutional convention, something allowed in the Constitution, and have the convention add language explicitly outlawing abortion. However, this was risky because there was no ironclad way to restrict such a convention and, given what was going on at the time in other state legislatures, it was starting to seem plausible that such a nightmare might become reality.

I had decided some days earlier to take a risk and beat Joanne to the punch and make my own motion to pull a bill. I had told no one. When the Speaker recognized me, I made a motion to pull from committee Bill 888 (*his* bill calling for a moratorium on the construction of nuclear power plants).

The Speaker looked mortified and yelled at Tom Melvin, the assistant chief clerk, who stood just below him on the imposing oak superstructure that culminated in the Speaker's perch, "What the hell is Assembly Bill 888?" "Melvie," as he was affectionately called, turned and looked up at the Speaker and said, slowly, savoring each word with a voice dripping with mock incredulity, "Why Ed, that's your bill."

THE DEMOCRATIC CAUCUS

As I had intended, my motion to pull a bill forced us into caucus to confront the "you don't pull bills" rule, and I knew this would quickly and naturally turn into a fight about Joanne's impending motion. I had upped the ante by making a motion to pull a bill introduced by the Speaker. The bill was one that the conservatives and the Republicans would vote to keep in committee, and the liberals and young Turks, once they figured out the internal dynamics and external politics, would, with no lack of glee, vote to schedule.

My motion turned the tables and demonstrated that a motion to pull a bill was not just something the pro-choice group could use to force its issue on to the agenda. Others could play this game, too.

It was understood that the nuclear power plant moratorium bill was a symbolic bill put forth by the Democratic leadership as a policy statement. It wasn't going anywhere. For years many of the young liberal Democrats in the legislature, including the Speaker and the majority leader, had feuded with the old guard leadership of the state AFL-CIO over three issues: building more freeways through Milwaukee, putting a deposit on beer cans, and, important for my purpose, nuclear power.

I was in effect saying that if the pro-choice leaders felt free to make a motion to pull their bill, and there were to be no repercussions for doing so, then the liberals had a few bills they would like to force onto the agenda. The nuclear power plant moratorium bill was just one of them.

Nobody really wanted to vote on the moratorium bill, which is why I had chosen it. I also wanted to force the Speaker to confront Joanne and the WCCL, something that was not likely to put me in his good graces. In the caucus, as the Speaker fulminated and the majority leader feigned a look of disgust, the members quickly figured out that a deal had to be struck. After being lectured by the Speaker about his bills, us, and our caucus, I said I would back down if Joanne also played by the rules and would forget about her motion. Joanne finally gave in to the group pressure, which quickly had shifted from me to her, and she said she would not make her motion for the good of "the Democrats." However, she wanted "something to be done." We all agreed to that and eagerly left the room.

AN ATTEMPT AT COMPROMISE

Something had to be done, but what? It was the same every session. The fight in the Assembly over taking up "the" abortion bill would rage behind the scenes and in the Democratic caucus, and finally, late in the session, after several threats to pull the bill, it would be scheduled, angrily debated, passed overwhelmingly, and then sent to the Senate with the expectation it would not be taken up before the legislature adjourned.

A legislative session is the two-year period between elections. During the session several floor periods are scheduled. The floor period is when all the members are on the floor of the Assembly or Senate to debate, amend, and vote on the bills that have come out of committee. In the first year of the session, the odd-numbered year, the legislature busied itself with passing the state budget. This took the spring floor period that started in February and ended on June 30. There was another floor period in October, and then a two-month spring floor period ending in April in the election year, and that was the end of the session for possible action on bills. So if the abortion bill was held in the Assembly for the first year, which it usually was, there was little time left in the session for the WCCL to force it to a vote in the Senate (given all the hurdles a bill must jump before it comes up for a vote). The bill would be killed if no vote was taken, and the process would have to start all over again the next session.

I was elected the majority leader in my third session, the same session that a compromise on the issue of abortion was tried. Almost seven months after the start of this session, Assembly Bill 621 was introduced. The bill, offered by Rep. Dismas Becker, a Democrat from Milwaukee and a former priest, proposed to prohibit late (second trimester) abortions from being performed in public hospitals. The WCCL was pushing a more stringent bill that prohibited all abortions in public hospitals.

Bill 621 was important because its sponsor, as the chairman of the Health and Human Services Committee, would decide whether any bills dealing with abortion would be reported to the floor. With his bill Dismas was trying to fend off the absolute restrictions in the WCCL bill. He believed that a compromise was actually possible if he worked at it. After all, he was the chair of the committee, and the two sides had to deal with him.

Perhaps a former Catholic priest could help bring the two sides together. Dismas was a class act. He had no guile and was respected on both sides of the aisle. He looked a little like Michelangelo's David, albeit older and in a creased gray suit. Dismas's district on the north side of Milwaukee was mostly Catholic and 25 percent black. Milwaukee votes Democratic, and a candidate who wins the primary is as good as elected. One of the areas Dismas had to pay attention to was the parish of Saint Sebastion Catholic Church. The four wards around Saint Sebastion outvoted the rest of Dismas's district in primary elections. Saint Sebastion was a very active and organized pro-life congregation. It was the church of WCCL lobbyist Barbara Lyons.

The bill to restrict abortions in public hospitals was a tough one for legislators to oppose because it was a tough one to explain. On the surface it appeared to end tax subsidies for second trimester abortions. In reality it eliminated any opportunity at all for late abortions. This was because the Wisconsin Medical Examining Board required all second trimester abortions to be performed in hospitals. The proposed definition of "public hospital" eliminated University Hospital and Madison General Hospital, the only two hospitals in the state where the procedure was performed. Thus, if the bill were to pass, elective abortions in the second trimester would not have been obtainable, even though they would have been legal.[1]

But try to explain all this to a constituent! "If you can't explain your

---

[1] In *Webster* v. *Reproductive Health* (1989), the U.S. Supreme Court upheld a Missouri definition of "public facility" that included hospitals on land leased from the state or any agency or political subdivision. Madison General Hospital is a private hospital located on land leased from the City of Madison. Memo entitled "Coverage of Madison General Hospital Under 1981 Assembly Bill 621" to Rep. Thomas A. Loftus from Richard Sweet, senior staff attorney, October 26, 1981.

position in thirty seconds, rethink your position." This is a motto many legislators live by. The "public hospital" bill had a lot of legislators re-thinking their position.

Dismas tried to be a peacemaker in the abortion wars. He once said, "As a committee chair, I tried to create alternatives that people could vote on that wouldn't do any damage. I could deal with the pro-life movement. I always left my door open to show where I was wrong. I wasn't hard on abortion."

However, even Dismas's patience wasn't going to move the WCCL and its allies in the Assembly away from their fight to win—to defeat the other side and have their position become the law of the land. The goal of the national right-to-life movement was to pass an extreme "public hospitals" statute in order to get a good test case before the U.S. Supreme Court that would present an opportunity to chip away at or perhaps reverse *Roe v. Wade*.

PASSAGE AND DEFEAT

Dismas did not succeed in getting his committee to report out a version of Assembly Bill 621 that met his professed criteria of doing "little damage." He had taken the unusual step of not soliciting co-sponsors of his bill, believing that if only his name was listed on the bill, it wouldn't be auto-matically catalogued as pro-life or pro-choice.

On the last day of the fall floor period, the last day for bills to be considered until the next year, debate began on Assembly Bill 621. I made a motion to reject amendment three, which, if adopted, would change the bill so it did what the WCCL wanted. I had no illusions about what was about to happen. My motion failed 34 to 64. At that point Dismas moved that the bill be withdrawn and returned to the author. He wanted "his" bill back because it no longer represented what he believed. It did a lot of damage. His request was denied, 68 to 30. The WCCL version of the bill was tacked on to Dismas's bill, and it passed 70 to 28. Dismas voted against passage.

The leadership in the Assembly did its job, however. The bill was held as long as possible, and the Senate, after holding four public hearings and fending off a motion to pull the bill, killed Assembly Bill 621 when it adjourned for the session the following April. "Something" was done, but nothing was passed, and the members survived another session of the abortion wars.

Although the legislature is designed to produce compromise, the pro-cess will not work if the issue is one where strong interest groups do not seek compromise, and the politicians can discern no point of consensus among their constituents. Abortion is also an issue where it is hard to be representative. I think all of us, Democrat or Republican, liberal or conservative, doubted our ability to represent others on the issue of abortion. We had the power to make decisions that could become law, but that didn't mean we had more wisdom than the rest of humankind.

The National Rifle Association: A Unique Interest Group

Gun control is an issue dominated by mindless passion and fear of voter reprisal.[1]

I am a former military policeman, medal winner with the Colt 45, and an owner of two shotguns. I know the destruction guns can bring, but I also know the joy they offer to the sportsman and collector.[2]

The first quote is from an editorial entitled "Pistol Lunacy." It was written in response to a gun control decision by the West Virginia Supreme Court in 1987. The court held that the state's concealed weapons law was unconstitutional. In particular, the law infringed on rights affirmed by the state in a recent amendment to its constitution, an amendment supported by the National Rifle Association (NRA) and adopted by the West Virginia legislature.

The second quote is the last paragraph of the letters I would send to NRA members who wrote to me. They were not friendly letters. I came to relish my fights against the NRA because, unlike most fights on legislative issues, I never gave any thought to an eventual compromise.

My attitude was that if the NRA lobbyists, who literally could direct dozens of votes in the legislature, wanted something from the Assembly, they would have to do it over my dead body (figuratively speaking). A fight with the NRA was baseball bats at close range, and I learned to swing first. During my fourteen years in the Wisconsin legislature, no serious

---

[1] *Gazette*, Charleston, West Virginia, May 20, 1987.
[2] Part of my standard written reply to members of the NRA who wrote to me.

attempt was ever made to enact any type of gun control legislation. Incredibly, given the carnage in our society caused by guns, such legislation had become nearly impossible to enact by the mid-1980s. All we could do was fight to hold onto the few restrictions on guns already in the law.

The National Rifle Association is a unique interest group because of the zeal of its members and the mythology of guns in America. For every interest group that wants something from the legislature, there is almost always a countervailing force—usually a competing interest group. This is not the case with the NRA. The press could exert countervailing pressure, but there has to be a story to report on for a war to be waged. The Speaker has the power, money, loyalty, and press attention to thwart a powerful interest group. But he or she will pay a political price if that group is the NRA.

THE NRA'S STRATEGY AND MINE

In the 1980s the NRA targeted several states. NRA members were urged to lobby the legislatures of these states to enact measures that would, in effect, repeal all local ordinances governing firearms and take the power to enact other gun laws away from cities, counties, and towns. In Wisconsin the NRA proposed amending the state's constitution to include this statement: "Every person has the right to keep and bear arms for security and defense, for lawful hunting and recreational use and for any other lawful purpose." [3] The NRA's goal was far-reaching. The amendment, it hoped, would provide the constitutional basis for the Wisconsin Supreme Court to strike down the state laws dealing with guns. (Just think of who "every person" includes.) The NRA knew what it was doing by proposing this constitutional amendment. Already several states, in addition to West Virginia, had added NRA-sponsored language to their constitutions.

I believed it was my job as Speaker to lead the fight against the NRA's legislation. And I consciously chose not to resist by directing from backstage, hidden in the labyrinth of rules and process I knew so well. In order to expose this powerful group to the sunlight of public debate, where it could be made to blink, like rats emerging from a sewer, the fight had to be made personal: them versus me, the NRA versus the Speaker. I knew they would accommodate me in the choice of battleground because they were reckless with their troops.

---

[3] Wisconsin Assembly, Joint Resolution 18, 1989.

GROWING UP WITH GUNS

I didn't run for the legislature with the idea that fighting the NRA would be part of the job. I grew up with guns. There was always a shotgun around, and pheasant hunting in the fall was as natural as the falling leaves. Even before I could carry a gun, I was taken along with the men, albeit more as an extra dog than as a hunter. After years of whining and begging my mother to allow me to have a gun, she relented. One Christmas a Daisy Red Ryder BB gun showed up under the tree. I also received dire warnings not to shoot someone's eye out. I was told to remember we lived in town, and guns weren't for town. (I did almost shoot my eye out when I missed my cardboard target in the basement and a BB ricocheted off a pipe.) In due time I was entrusted with the ownership of a single-shot 410 and later with a sixteen-gauge Remington pump.

Hunting was another chance to go to my uncle's farm and see my cousins and tear through the sheds and the hay mow and the barn, where we would ride the calves. The hunting was always with my father, Adolph; his brother, Edward; and Ed's neighbor, Earl Brown. We would amble through Ed's farm, where my father had grown up, and then down to my Aunt Mildred's to hunt the big marsh. These were glorious, festival-like days, made for dogs and kids, days that were sunny and crisp. My dad would talk Norwegian with his sisters at the big lunch at Mildred's. Later, outside by the barn, the men would pass a tin of Copenhagen and sneak a swallow of blackberry brandy from Ed's pint. The kids could see this, but not the women. We never told.

The hunt would end at milking time for Ed, but the day's fun would continue in the tiny farm village of Brooklyn at the Anchor Club tavern (no telephone, parking in back). There the other hunters and more cousins would be bursting to tell the stories of their day. The kids could have candy bars, and I got my dad's pool cue on every fourth shot. We heard the stories, over and over again, of the time on our farm when my dad shot pheasants for the hunters from Chicago, and the time in high school when he out-pitched Johnny Saxer, who later played for the university. The green Studebaker with the V8 engine would bring us home, and my mother would be happy that we were safe and my dad had given the pheasants away. And I was happy she didn't have to clean them because that was work she did on the farm and we were in town now.

NRA-STYLE LOBBYING

The event that gave the NRA its current essence, and at once provided its rallying cry, occurred in Morton Grove, Illinois, where an ordinance was enacted that outlawed the *possession* of handguns in the village. The specter of this act gave the NRA the idea and the excuse for starting a nationwide campaign to prohibit local governments from enacting Morton Grove-type ordinances.

The NRA followed more or less the same tactics in all state legislatures. It would have its lead minion in the legislature introduce a bill. Then, in a special "letter" to its members, it would cry wolf and rave about an impending doom that could be avoided only if members took immediate action. The recommended action was a telephone call to the member's local legislator. Calling at night was recommended because that was the surest way to reach the person. Obligingly, the NRA provided the legislator's phone number. It also provided the villain's phone number. There was always a hero and a villain.

By the 1989-90 session I was firmly established as the villain. I had beat the NRA lobbyists the previous session, but they thought that this time I was vulnerable. My all-but-declared candidacy for governor might give them an edge, they hoped. The NRA didn't want to lose again. Its frustration showed in the barking rhetoric of the special letter it sent to its members in October 1989.[4] A few excerpts follow:

> Help Preserve Your Firearms Freedom in Wisconsin—Support Assembly Bill 244 and Assembly Joint Resolution 18.
>
> URGENT! Your help is needed—and needed now—to preserve your Right to Keep and Bear Arms in Wisconsin for today and in the future. . . .
>
> By acting today . . . you can help ensure the future of your firearms freedom in Wisconsin. By failing to take action, towns and cities across the state will have an open invitation to follow the lead of Morton Grove. . . .

The straining, squealing quality of the NRA's practiced rhetoric always reminded me of a pip-squeak second lieutenant dressing down a private. The letter went on to give the NRA's version of the fight it had lost in the last session and issued a call to arms, or at least to telephones.

> You may recall in 1988, a bill similar to A.B. 244, which prohibited the passage of "Morton Grove-type" handgun bans, passed the House and Senate with wide support. The bill should have been sent to the Governor for action. Yet anti-gun Speaker Loftus sent the bill to a special conference committee. . . . Loftus packed the committee with his anti-

---

[4] National Rifle Association of America, Institute for Legislative Action, 1600 Rhode Island Avenue, N.W., Washington, D.C. 20036. Newsletter dated October 18, 1989.

gun cronies who rewrote the bill, stripping it of the key provisions protecting Wisconsin sportsmen. . . .

Throughout this brutal legislative battle, Speaker Loftus displayed his hatred for firearm owners and disdain for your Right to Keep and Bear Arms. Loftus, one man standing alone, thwarted the will of the legislature and the will of the people.

Don't Let Speaker Loftus Pull Another Hatchet Job Before He Steps Down As Speaker in 1991!

Call Speaker Loftus today . . . and politely urge him to stop standing in the way of passage of A.B. 244 and A.J.R. 18.

By 1989 there was nothing "polite" about our shootouts. It was what the NRA didn't tell its members about the previous showdown during the 1987-88 session that really galled me.

THE BATTLE OVER MORTON GROVE

The battlefield was the state Assembly and Senate's conference committee on the budget bill. I was the Assembly chairman of the committee and appointed the other two Assembly members. The committee replaced the NRA language in the bill, which repealed all local gun laws and forbid the enactment of new ones, with language specifically prohibiting local ordinances from banning handguns. In this way we thought we exorcised the "Morton Grove" bogeyman in Wisconsin. The next session proved us wrong.

Despite what it might say, the NRA did not want a law prohibiting local ordinances from banning handguns. If the language it was howling for was adopted, the NRA would not achieve the real purpose of the campaign—to nullify the local restrictions on guns currently in effect and to prohibit (under state law) cities, villages, and towns from enacting any gun ordinances in the future. It would be difficult to rally the troops for this real goal after the symbolic enemy had been vanquished. "Morton Grove" could no longer serve as the raw meat to move its members to action.

My co-conspirator, Rep. Dave Travis from Madison, and I knew that the NRA would have to use up some chips with Republican governor Tommy Thompson to get him to veto this provision, even though it did exactly what the NRA said it wanted done (namely, prohibit local ordinances from banning handguns). Tommy Thompson was a long-time supporter of the NRA, which had been helpful in his campaign for governor, so a veto was likely. I thought that there was a slim chance the governor would let the language stand. I knew that he could figure out that this "victory" in Wisconsin would make the NRA shift its lobbying effort elsewhere, to other target states, and could save him some trouble down the road.

By 1989 guns had become a big issue again. Throughout the country crazy people were gunning down their neighbors with their mail order Uzis, and in Milwaukee the murder rate had reached a record high. Each murder had become part of a well-reported count. The biggest press splash was the day, relatively early in the year, that the old record was surpassed.[5]

The image the people of Milwaukee had of their town as a rather safe place was shattered. One of the television stations led its news each night with a graphic showing a chalk outline of a body. The message was clear: the day was another day of gunfire in the city. Milwaukee, it seemed, was becoming one more big city with big city problems.

The police and city politicians called for stricter controls on guns. They put forth rather Milquetoast measures, but the atmosphere was right for something to be done. The focus of attention was on blacks in the inner city, where an epidemic of gun violence raged.

Scared by black-on-black violence, white people in Milwaukee became really alarmed when Alderman Michael McGee threatened violence by 1995 if the white power structure didn't throw several hundred million dollars at the inner city. He hypothesized about snipers shooting at freeway commuters driving home to the suburbs and about attacks on corporate boxes at Milwaukee Bucks basketball games.

McGee dominated the news. He had the visual menace and sound bite rhetoric made for TV (he was on *Donahue*). In his fatigues and beard, he looked like Castro. He made statements that scared the hell out of whites (for example, boasting about how he learned to shoot in Vietnam). He wore a military holster strapped to his hip. There was no gun in the holster, but with the leather flap over its top, you couldn't really tell.

With the murders in Milwaukee and the ominous image of Michael McGee with a gun, the governor might have a hard time signing a bill that eliminated all the city's gun laws and restricted its ability to enact other restrictions. Why not go along with the game and sign the anti-Morton Grove law and take away the main lever the NRA had to do future mis-

---

[5] There were 116 murders in the city of Milwaukee in 1989. This record high was surpassed in 1990 (165 murders) and again in 1991 (166 murders). The 166th murder in 1991 occurred on December 31, when a seventeen-year-old boy was shot and killed by another youth who tried to steal his Chicago Bulls basketball jacket. *Milwaukee Sentinel*, December 31, 1991.

chief? However, in a low bow to the NRA, the governor vetoed the part of the budget bill containing the anti-Morton Grove language.

WHY LEGISLATORS GIVE IN TO THE NRA

Giving in to a powerful interest group with a narrow agenda is almost a natural instinct of legislators. For many it is just not worth the political pain to fight, or even reason with, a group like the NRA. Furthermore, why invite trouble during your next campaign, or even risk your political career, by provoking the NRA? After all, not a great deal of harm would be done if the NRA got its way. (Could there possibly be more guns available?) Someone else would fight the fight. Furthermore, wasn't it the job of the leaders to shape the language in a bill so no real damage would be done if there ever was a vote?

Every member I served with had a boundary in his or her mind—a line the member would not cross regardless of the political consequences. This boundary was drawn where right or wrong was at stake. Usually this question came when debating issues that skirted the edges of constitutional guarantees. For example, debates on bills on abortion, obscenity, civil rights, and due process became debates on the "freedoms." Each legislator had a strong opinion about where the authors of the U.S. Constitution intended the limits to be placed.

However, the intent of the framers concerning guns is certainly not clear in the Constitution. And hardly any politician is willing to voluntarily tell the extremists in the NRA that they are nut cases. If you see an accident, you slow down and put on your seat belt, and legislators had seen enough of the NRA's clout to become cautious. The openness of my fight with NRA lobbyists was seen as temerity by many, but I felt the time was right to take them on since their extremism had made them a public relations disaster throughout the country, and I had won round one in the 1987-88 session. The fight that session ended with the NRA lobbyists on the mat, forced to spend political capital asking the governor to veto what they ostensibly wanted. I had also demonstrated how to fight the NRA, or at least how a legislative leader could fight the NRA. But I paid a price.

ASSAULT BY TELEPHONE

I never installed an answering machine or employed an answering service for my home phone until I declared my candidacy for governor. I wanted my constituents to be able to call me directly. I was always pleased when I answered, and the caller would say, "Oh, I didn't expect to get you." It wasn't all altruism since little things like this translated into votes.

Things changed when the NRA identified me as the anti-gun devil and provided my telephone number to its 80,000 members. Like zombies programmed to call, the NRA true believers dialed my number one after another, and the phone started to ring nonstop. If I picked up the receiver and immediately put it down, a new ring would start with another call. If I said hello, it was like tripping open a talking jack-in-the-box, as the voice at the other end would start to mouth the spiel provided in the NRA newsletter. Trying to converse was usually out of the question. Their mission was to deliver a message, and they did not want me to paint any gray on their black and white view of gun legislation.

When you are elected to office you start to tolerate fools. It is because each opinion is supposed to count, and each caller or letter writer is a potential vote. This isn't irrational. While campaigning for governor, I often would hear a comment from someone whose opinion of me was based on a letter I had sent to the person years earlier. The politician's voice of caution is like a little winged fairy that constantly whispers, "Caution, potential vote." Think of Tinkerbell on your shoulder with a poll list on a clip board.

One of the stitches that holds representative government together is the politician who, after receiving a letter that starts out "You idiot! I'll never vote for you again," actually replies and begins the return letter by saying, "Thank you for your letter. I respect your position." A free stamp is essential to the latter half of this equation.

My wife did not tolerate incivility. Our second child, Karl, was still a baby when the NRA phone campaign began, and the late night calls would invariably wake Karl and start him crying. Barbara would pick up the phone and not waiting for the man—it was a always a man—to start his monologue would say, "You should be ashamed of yourself. There is a baby here trying to sleep. Don't you know what time it is? If you want to contact Tom, you write him at the Capitol. You can write, can't you?" And the receiver would smash down with a force that made me think deep thoughts about the strength of plastic.

Some of the callers were nice and would apologize for the NRA tactics and sincerely state their case. Some worried for my political welfare and, in a fatherly manner, urged me to get out of harm's way. But the calls to my home were incessant, as were the calls and letters to my office.

OTHER TACTICS BY THE NRA

A lot of interest groups have a big membership list and use newsletters to exhort their members to contact their legislators. The NRA, however, has zealots that really call, and they call every time they are asked. Not big labor, not big business, not environmental groups, not teachers, not trial lawyers, and not even chiropractors have such obedient followers. And if a legislator was at a plant gate, or a parade, there would be the more than occasional comment about guns or a shout, "No gun control!"

Worst of all was if someone brought up your NRA roll call voting. Were you graded "A"? Did you pass? Some of my colleagues had the sinking suspicion that the comments at the plant gates, the calls, and the letters all were part of a secret society with a Grand Dragon and a funny handshake. Not knowing how many members there were, they kept their heads down when the subject of guns came up in the legislature.

Just before the official start of my campaign for governor in 1990, I was at the home of Rep. Virgil Roberts near La Crosse. He had arranged for me to speak to a small-business group. Virgil checked the answering machine before we left the house for the trip. We stood together and listened to the tape as someone describing himself as an old friend of Virgil's said, "Virgil, I know you have been with us before and you're OK on guns, but this Loftus guy is not letting our gun bill get a vote. You need to help us. I've been a Democrat but Loftus better change on guns."

I had put Virgil, and many other Democrats, in a tough spot. They had to defend me and make excuses for me. Part of their support for me was partisan, much of it was friendship, and some of it was solidarity with one who stands up to the bully.

I had started to collect a list of NRA members from those who called or wrote to me. I also kept a different list (not as long) of those who supported my position. This list included quite a few people who wrote about their experiences as crime victims or about how their families had been destroyed by some gun incident (usually the accidental shooting of a child). And I had developed a list of potential allies, mostly police and prosecutors, who, if they knew what was going on, might help in the fight.

Little press attention was given to the "gun fights" in the legislature. They simply weren't reported because they were "process"—legislative maneuvering rather than an isolated story that fit the "this-happened-today" criteria of newspapers. I had started to fix this by creating events, quotes, and public controversy. I had learned some things, and my experience would prove to be crucial. But mostly the fight was not public. Unreported by the press, the NRA chased its bill from committee to committee.

ROUND ONE: ASSEMBLY BILL 76

The first fight with the NRA had culminated in the veto of the anti-Morton Grove language from the budget bill at the end of the session in 1988. The fight ended this way, but it started and was fought—with procedural moves and counterpunching in the newspapers—over Assembly Bill 76. This bill would have repealed all local guns restrictions and stripped municipalities of the power to regulate guns at all.

Throughout 1987 and 1988 I had shuffled Assembly Bill 76 from committee to committee until finally, with less than a month to go before final adjournment, the only choice left for the NRA was to try to schedule the bill with a motion that required a two-thirds vote.

Assembly Bill 76 was introduced on January 3, 1987, and I referred it to the Committee on Urban and Local Affairs. I told the chairman to sit on the bill (in other words, never let the committee vote on it). The chairman, Spencer Coggs, was a savvy guy and the chairman the NRA would have the least influence over. He represented a district torn by violence in the heart of Milwaukee.

Most bills can be held in committee for the first year of a two-year session. After this unofficial grace period, the pressure for action builds. During the second year Democratic legislators were being barraged by NRA phone calls asking them to help move the bill, and I knew I had to make some concession. Therefore, on February 9, 1988, I worked a deal to move Assembly Bill 76 from the Urban and Local Affairs Committee to a friendlier committee. It was unlikely that this chairman would hold it, but I was using time, keeping the bill moving, hoping a vote would not be scheduled before the session adjourned on April 5th.

That chairman weathered exactly two days of phone calls before he scheduled a hearing and a vote. On February 23rd the bill was approved 7 to 0. I said to hell with it to myself and, in a rarely used move, referred the bill again, this time to the Joint Finance Committee. This was a diabolical yet just move since the Assembly co-chairman, Rep. Marlin Schneider, was the most rabid in his belief in the sanctity of unhampered access to guns in America. It was giving the bill to the chairman that loved it most, but he would have to use precious time to schedule a vote and report it out. This made the NRA, and Marlin, livid.

The bill was almost dead now since the Senate was very unlikely to act, even on this bill, given the little time left. In twenty-one days it wouldn't matter, the last days of the session were firmly under the control of the leadership, and the members would soon be consumed by the budget and concentrating on slicing election-year bacon.

Democrats Marlin Schneider and Bob Thompson, the two members of the Assembly who led the fight for NRA legislation, were having fits over what they considered my unfairness. When I referred the bill to the Finance Committee, forcing a few more days to be wasted while Marlin rounded up the votes to get it out of his own committee, it was the last straw. The showdown came in the caucus.

THE RANK-AND-FILE PROTEST

Marlin blew up that day in caucus (he blew up most days) and threatened to make a motion to pull the bill from his own committee. I said any Democrat voting to schedule this bill would "have hell to pay," and for added drama I started to walk out of the room. I didn't get far. My colleagues weren't about to let me put them in this bind: vote yes and incur my wrath, vote no and go on the NRA's most wanted list. Amid much shouting, I returned to the front of the room to make the case against the NRA that I had been planning.

The previous week an NRA mailing had caused phones to ring, including mine. I talked to the Democrats like the leader of the defenders of a city under siege. "My family has been harassed with incessant late night phone calls." (So had their families.) "The NRA is threatening to work against me if I run for governor unless I roll over on this insane bill." (They were being threatened also.) "If you let them set the schedule, they will own you." (They were already rented.) "Marlin, you have your precious bill in your own committee, kick it out." (Catch this: Marlin wants to make a motion to pull a bill from his own committee.) "Don't put the rest of us through the cut and give the NRA a roll call on some procedural motion." (What are you anyway? A fifth columnist?) Marlin relented but scheduled a quick committee vote.

This caucus generated the first real news story on gun control in some time. At last reporters had something to cover besides legislative maneuvering on gun control bills. Something happened involving the Speaker and the NRA, powerful and quotable political players. "Gun bill triggers angry debate," said the *Milwaukee Journal*.[6] "NRA targets state passage of bill limiting gun control," said Madison's *Capital Times*.[7] And the press knew there was more news to come. The caucus was on March 7th, and the session was scheduled to end April 5th.

MORE COMMITTEES TAKE A LOOK

On March 9th the Finance Committee acted, adding some amendments that allowed regulations currently in effect (for example, bans on taking loaded guns into bars, public buildings, and on school buses) but prohibiting any future restrictions. This made the bill less loony, but it violated the purity the NRA wanted. However, the NRA had succeeded in adding an amendment calling for a $20,000 gun safety study. This amend-

---

[6] *Milwaukee Journal*, March 9, 1988.
[7] *Capital Times*, March 9, 1988.

ment made the bill an "appropriations bill," and the governor could veto parts of money bills. This amendment was "insurance" for the NRA. If the bill happened to pass as it came out of committee, the NRA would ask the governor to veto all parts of the bill it didn't like. After adding the amendment, the committee voted to send the bill out for scheduling on a vote of 13 to 2.

The bill came out on March 14th, and I referred it to the Rules Committee, which was the scheduling committee. Chaired by Majority Leader Tom Hauke, the Rules Committee was composed of the leadership. Tougher than nails, he jumped in every foxhole I found myself in, including this one. The committee did not schedule bills objected to by the Speaker.

I was hoping that we could hold the bill and was busy suggesting that the bill was too controversial to take up this late in the session. "I've got to believe that the bill is dead. We don't have time to take up the thousands of bills laying around like this one that are all botched up." [8]

One NRA lobbyist had a different view. "It is not a dead issue. As far as I'm concerned, he's against the Wisconsin sportsman. The one million plus people who buy hunting licenses are not going to be very happy. We're running out of time. If it gets to the floor, it will be passed." [9] The NRA lobbyist was right about the latter point. The modifying amendments would be stripped, and the bill would pass if it reached the floor.

The bill could sit in the Rules Committee for three weeks before it could be pulled by a simple majority vote, leaving the forces of darkness with the prospect of mustering a two-thirds vote to force the issue. This wasn't going to happen. There just weren't sixty-six sheep among the ninety-nine members of the Assembly. (The herd probably hovered at a tad more than fifty on this vote.)

This activity was occurring during the fast and furious last weeks of the session. We were also considering a special annual budget bill, so the normal end-of-session chaos was intensified. It was the time of supreme control for me, but to the rest I must have looked like Zeus directing a blizzard of cats.

NRA's Radio Blitz

The NRA lobbyists had had it, and they started to run radio spots aimed at me.

Once again Speaker Tom Loftus is trying to close the door on Wisconsin

---

[8] Tom Loftus, quoted by the Associated Press, March 9, 1988.
[9] Robert Faulkner, quoted by the Associated Press, March 10, 1988.

sportsmen. He's vowed to kill Assembly Bill 76 that preserves your right to keep and bear arms. Even though AB 76 won overwhelming support in committees, Loftus is now the one man keeping your firearms freedoms from a fair floor vote. Call him today at the Capitol and ask for a vote on AB 76 before Loftus does it again. Paid for by the 80,000 Wisconsin NRA members.[10]

The day after the ad started to run, a Republican legislator made the motion to pull the bill from the Rules Committee. No Democrat could be found to make the motion to pull the bill. Tom Hauke, who had been waiting to engage the enemy, like a big gun kept in reserve, thundered with institutional indignation and railed against the very idea that anyone with a backbone would vote with the NRA. He said, "This state legislature doesn't make deals with Washington, D.C. We don't cave in to pressure, and we don't cave in to threats in this Legislature." [11] This was news to me, but Tom was serious and the Democrats knew it. Better to cave in on another day. To our surprise, the vote failed 59 to 37.

Tom Hauke had a Brando-like half smile and the solid look of a compact fighter. Like a boxer waiting for the bell, he stood at his position, the corner of the Democratic aisles in the front of the chamber. His workman-like, never uncertain, handling of the majority leader's job was a pleasant surprise to all of us, because Tom, although a veteran of sixteen years, had spent his career as a maverick. Tom had worked his way through Marquette Law School and represented the working town of West Allis. He had street smarts, a conservative instinct, and the knowledge, education, and guts to take on power. It was as if he drew a line in the sand and dared political bullies, "Just try and cross."

ENLISTING THE PRESS

After the failed vote to pull Assembly Bill 76, I continued to hammer away at the NRA lobbyists and their tactics:

> I think the NRA should apologize to the Legislature and come back next session and play by the rules. After the apology, maybe we'll start in January with a clean slate.[12]

My press strategy was to avoid attacking NRA members but to fire

---

[10] Script of NRA ad that played on various radio stations throughout the state from March 15, 1988, to March 19, 1988.

[11] *Wisconsin State Journal*, March 16, 1988.

[12] This quote is from an Associated Press story that appeared in state papers on March 16, 1988, the day after the vote. The headline in the *Capital Times* was "Lawmakers Blast NRA Tactics."

away at the group's "lobbyists" (always using that word). I accused them of misleading members on the real impact of Assembly Bill 76. I called them big boys from Washington who were just using the local innocents, the Wisconsin NRA members, as fodder in their campaign of extremism. I always wanted the reporters to get a quote from someone who would be identified as the NRA lobbyist. The *Milwaukee Sentinel* put it this way in a story headlined "Angry Legislators Resist NRA Barrage":

> Loftus had been the target of intensive lobbying by the NRA, which handed out his home telephone number to its 80,000 state members and is running a radio ad in his district urging people to contact him about the bill.
> "Their method of operation is tolerated in other states, but it isn't here," Loftus said. "They have no shame about misleading their own members."
>
> Bob Faulkner, Wisconsin field representative for the NRA, said later that Loftus "has chosen to run roughshod" over Assembly supporters of the bill. The NRA, he said, "is 80,000 people in Wisconsin that vote and each of those 80,000 people has five friends they go hunting with. Apparently, Tom Loftus doesn't realize that." [13]

I started to tip off my colleagues on what to expect by saying in the press that I would support a pure anti-Morton Grove bill. I wanted the Democrats to know that there would be an out that they could use if it became necessary. The press helped me publicize my view:

> Loftus said the NRA had misrepresented the bill to its members by maintaining it was aimed at warding off handgun bans of the type adopted by Morton Grove, Ill. "I support a bill that would ban Morton Grove ordinances in Wisconsin," Loftus said. But the original AB 76, he noted, even would have prevented cities from setting regulations against discharging firearms within city limits or carrying loaded guns into taverns. [14]

I used the press to communicate with the members of the legislature, the governor, and lobbyists. (This is another reason why the print press is so important in state legislatures.) Communication was facilitated by our in-house newsletter, *Capital Headlines*. It was distributed daily and consisted of clips from the two Milwaukee and two Madison papers.

The two Madison papers, the morning *Wisconsin State Journal* and the afternoon *Capital Times*, covered the legislature extensively because Madison is the state capital and because of their readership of state and university employees. The morning *Milwaukee Sentinel* had clout because it

---

[13] *Milwaukee Sentinel*, March 16, 1988.
[14] Associated Press, March 16, 1988.

played up state political news, and it was distributed statewide. Unless you could make a splash in the Sunday edition, the afternoon *Milwaukee Journal* wasn't much of a player since the stories were not timely, and the paper had started to focus on suburban news. The thin edition distributed statewide was day-old news sold as a morning paper (the sunrise edition), and the editorials were a hopeless mishmash of mugwump mush in the tone of parental lectures that produced nothing much other than groans.

MY NEWSMAKING STRATEGY

The main impact of the NRA radio attack was to create a news story and give me another opportunity to appear like Davy Crockett at the Alamo. Like the Alamo defenders, I was ever vigilant in looking for opportunities to land a cannonball on someone's head in the opposing camp. Fortunately, a "personal attack" rule of the Federal Communications Commission gave me an opening. The rule seemed to require that the radio stations give me an opportunity to respond to the NRA ad.[15]

If the Speaker sends a legal-sounding letter to the local radio station and asks for free response time (and the attacker is the NRA rather than the Pope, for example), that letter will ruin the station manager's day. So I was given a couple of spots, and the station defended itself against the NRA by saying this was just done for "fairness." My goal was to create another news story and get my response in the papers. The response ad was written to be read in the newspapers (very few people would hear it on the radio) and to restate some themes:

> This is Assembly Speaker Tom Loftus. Ask yourself, would you support a bill to repeal all local ordinances dealing with firearms and take away from communities their own power to propose another ordinance? Neither would I. Yet the NRA lobbyists, through letters and radio ads, mislead the public and their members, trying to fool them into believing that they lobbied only for a bill dealing with the ownership of guns. I'm sticking to my guns. There is no need to put stock in a group whose lobbyists mislead its own members.[16]

The radio ad response story played on the front page of the *Milwaukee Sentinel* with a picture. The heading was "Loftus fires back at NRA radio ads."[17]

I had made sure the editorial writers were following the gun fight in

---

[15] Federal Communications Commission, Rule C.F.R. 73.1920.

[16] The text of the response played over WTSO and WZEE radio in Madison. See also letter from Assembly Speaker Tom Loftus to Station Manager Roger Russell, March 17, 1988.

[17] *Milwaukee Sentinel*, April 6, 1988.

the legislature by sending them everything I could get my hands on to make my case, making sure they had quotes and understood the process. The NRA was having a bad week in the headlines: "NRA tactics are wrong," "NRA backed bill is irresponsible," "Showdown in Legislature leaves gun lobby wounded."[18]

THE MORTON GROVE VETO

The 1987-88 session ended well for our side. The NRA lobbyists had to scramble to persuade pro-gun legislators to sign a letter asking the governor to strike the anti-Morton Grove language from the budget. Ironically, the lobbyists had to push their followers back through their own kafkaesque maze of reasoning, trying to explain that what they had asked for was not what they wanted. After placing the Speaker against the wall, the NRA ended up shooting blanks. A firing squad with popguns. Marlin Schneider summed it up: "The NRA's rough lobbying tactics backfired when it tried to target Assembly Speaker Tom Loftus as the villain. They should understand the Legislature is like a fraternity. The pack pulls together if one member is attacked by an outside group."[19]

ROUND TWO: THE CONSTITUTIONAL AMENDMENT

In the 1989-90 session the issue changed to the NRA-backed constitutional amendment, and expectations changed. I had won one battle, and I would probably win again. I had been the Speaker for six years and was starting an unprecedented fourth term as Wisconsin's longest-serving Speaker.

Democrats in the legislature had remained in the majority in the 1980s even though we were at the foot of the ballot during the two Reagan landslides. We had survived the 1988 elections when the Republicans had outspent us two and three to one, with the governor shaking the money tree for his party like never before. In addition, I had accomplished what I had set out to do as Speaker: conduct myself with a civility of spirit, letting each legislator go his or her own way largely without criticism. I knew this would bring us closer and allow me the leeway to lead. I had given most Democrats the responsibility they asked for, supported them in their independence, and kept my door open to all political prodigals.

Early in 1989 there were calls for bans on assault rifles after the

---

[18] *Sheboygan Press*, March 18, 1988; *La Crosse Tribune*, March 21, 1988; and *Milwaukee Journal*, March 24, 1988.

[19] *Milwaukee Journal*, March 24, 1988.

schoolyard killings in Stockton, California. Proposals were put forth in Wisconsin, and the NRA started to whine, "We know of no way to protect sportsmen if an assault rifle ban were enacted." I didn't know what was coming, but I kept with the plan and responded: "Their lobbyists make a travesty of the position of their members. They twist the legitimate desire that Americans have to own and use weapons into something perverse. The NRA's tactics could turn off rather than sway the public." [20]

Sure enough, the issue did not become assault rifles, or any other proposal to curb guns; it became a fight over whether or not to add a "right to bear arms" clause to the constitution. If adopted, this amendment would weaken the legal basis for current state laws regulating guns.

In late 1989 as my race for governor was gearing up, James Hayes, the NRA lobbyist assigned to Wisconsin, telephoned my campaign director and hinted that a deal might be possible: the gun stuff passes, and the NRA pulls its punches in the governor's reelection campaign. Like Claude Rains who acted shocked when told there was gambling in Rick's Cafe, I feigned indignance that a legislative matter had been even discussed with campaign people. I fired off a letter promising not to "compromise my principles, or my opposition to the NRA's repealer bill regardless of the political capital you've offered." [21] I also accused Mr. Hayes of violating our lobby laws, threw in some legal citations, and made sure reporters had the letter in their hands just in time for the morning deadlines. It was important that this be an incident and become part of the legislative and press lore.

Then I began a letter-writing campaign to district attorneys, police chiefs, sheriffs, and even town constables. I explained how the routine powers they now employed in gun crimes would be compromised by the NRA proposal to amend the constitution. Since so little was known about the impact of the NRA bill, I did not mince words in these letters. Here's a sample:

> Although I am not for gun control, I am not for lunacy. The NRA lobbyist, Jim Hayes, is pushing a constitutional amendment that has been a disaster in other states. . . . In West Virginia the supreme court ruled that anyone over 21 can carry a concealed weapon without a permit. . . . In Maine a judge ruled that a convicted felon has the right to own firearms. . . . This resolution is being proposed in Wisconsin.[22]

Many wrote back and expressed incredulity that the legislature could

---

[20] From an Associated Press story appearing on March 22, 1989.

[21] Letter from me to James T. Hayes, National Rifle Association, Washington D.C., November 2, 1989.

[22] Partial text of a letter sent to law enforcement personnel on January 16, 1990.

even contemplate the NRA-backed change to the constitution. All these responses were compiled and sent to the NRA members I had been collecting on my list, as well as to legislators, editors, and the list of law enforcement people. The day before one crucial vote, I sent by Federal Express a letter asking the law enforcement people to call their legislators. Most of them did. With some lists, staff, and an unlimited budget for printing and postage (enjoyed only by the Speaker), I generated enough activity to keep the NRA on the defense. At least I kept their lips moving while they read my stuff.

For the public hearing on the NRA constitutional amendment, I brought in a Republican state senator from Nebraska. He talked about his state's trouble after the NRA-backed constitutional amendment had passed there. I flew in the police chief from Portland, Maine, to explain the troubles a right-to-bear-arms amendment had caused for the police in that state. And I made the head of the Wisconsin police chiefs' association come to present his group's opposition to the bill. I had asked him to wear his uniform and then made damn sure we appeared together on TV.

EPILOGUE

The NRA's repealer bill did not pass, nor did the right-to-bear-arms constitutional amendment it was pushing. The lobbyists' tactics and extremism has won the NRA press criticism and public disgust. Nevertheless, no opposing interest group has emerged. This absent watch dog would be compensated for if the NRA agenda was opposed by one of the political parties. But neither political party has an intelligent thing to say about guns. The press is pretty good at focusing on the NRA's bully-boy tactics and radical agenda but only if there is a story to tell.

Many of my colleagues, newcomers and veterans alike, didn't have a clue as to who the capital press were and how they operated. If legislators would simply ask each reporter who he or she worked for and what their deadlines were, most of the mystery of the press would be gone. If they then understood a story is an event and some quotes, they would be on their way to becoming talk show regulars. To create news in an effort to enlist the press in a fight politicians are fearful of undertaking is not easy. However, in our system no interest group should go unchecked, and the press is the NRA's only effective foil.

Child Support:
The Long March to Reform

A major change in a law is rarely accomplished in one legislative session. Several sessions usually are required to refine an idea and educate the members of the legislature. If the change will have an impact on the daily lives and rights of a lot of people, the idea must be sold outside the legislature to the groups affected. Changing the child support system is a particularly delicate matter because it affects laws dealing with divorce, paternity, and welfare. Child support laws specify the financial obligations of parents for their children after divorce or in the case of out-of-wedlock births.

Divorce often means the children and the mother end up on welfare because adequate financial support of the children comes to an end. This happens because the family that shared housing and income comes to an end, and the child support that may be received is simply not enough to replace it.

Child support is not welfare, but it is entwined with the politics of welfare in a state legislature. The welfare debate, inside and outside legislatures, has a lot to do with who should be eligible for a check from the government for living expenses. The question has become, "Who are the 'deserving poor' and what should they get?" When child support isn't paid, or isn't paid in full—the norm in America—those children and their mothers end up on welfare.

If one knows about welfare in America, one knows about America. Our democracy is about equality, and the poor are reminders of failure. The programs for the poor are designed to reflect the way things should be and the way people should be, not the way they are.

Welfare reform is an oxymoron in politics, and most legislators carry some rhetorical stick to keep it away from them. In the Wisconsin legislature the conservatives lamented welfare as a stipend to the lazy while saying kind things about the truly deserving. The liberals would blame something, like racism, for causing poverty in the first place.

This chapter tells the fourteen-year story of change in Wisconsin's child support laws. The quest started out in an unremarkable way—yet another attempt at welfare reform by yet another group. The quest ended, however, with significant change: the Wisconsin legislature enacted a new child support system, one that became the model for a new national law. A more radical part of the plan was rejected, but the idea favorably impressed the governor of Arkansas, who later became president.

THE COMMITTEE WITH JURISDICTION

When I was first elected to the legislature, I asked the Speaker to be named to the Health and Social Services Committee, the committee with jurisdiction over welfare and health care. He granted my request, and the committee turned out to be a great place. Through the committee's public hearings marched a parade of earnest supplicants asking us to help their cause followed by those doing their best to either fatten or protect their wallets. Hundreds of people attended these hearings. The issues—among them abortion and the licensing of medical professionals—were so intractable that my colleagues and I found ourselves in the role of referees. The members of the committee were a self-selected bunch. They wanted to be on this committee. They knew the job would bring some political headaches—if you pleased one group, you alienated another, especially with the abortion bills—but they cared about the issues, and this meant a camaraderie existed that crossed partisan lines.

The Committee Chairman

The chairman of the Health and Social Services Committee was Joe Czerwinski from the south side of Milwaukee. Joe was often called the Polish Prince ("Sir Winski"), and it was only partly because of his name. He was a dapper man who carried himself with a slim elegance, like Fred Astaire. He had a black Mercedes, albeit the small four-door model; it lacked hubcaps, and the wiper on the passenger side was stuck at half-wipe. We were both in our early thirties, and we became best of friends.

The committee chair in the vast majority of state legislatures has control of the agenda. Thus he or she decides what bills to bring up for a public hearing, and whether to then hold a vote that would report them out for floor action. The committee is the duchy, the bills are the subjects, and the chair is the duke or the duchess. (In this case a prince.)

Joe never let a bill out of his committee unless it was in a form ready to be passed into law. He made the competing interest groups compromise, and he got the committee members, both Democrats and Republicans, to support what the committee did. If a bill, like an abortion bill, had to come out of the committee and no position could be reached that could be held on the floor, Joe stuck to the best version, and made those who would amend it work hard and pay a price later for going against the committee. Even then, when the plan was to lose, but hold as much ground as possible, he made sure that it was his okay that seemed to count. When I became Speaker and started to appoint the chairs of committees, I would consciously make my decisions based on whether they would likely meet the Joe Czerwinski test on bills referred to their committee for care.

THE SUBCOMMITTEE

When in doubt or when in political need, form a committee. Welfare, always an issue, was percolating on the political front burner because of the state's generous welfare payments, nearly the highest in the country, and the escalating costs of the state's "Cadillac" Medicaid program. Medicaid was the extensive health insurance coverage that came with eligibility for welfare, and its costs were skyrocketing right along with other health care costs. There was a clamor to "do something." Joe Czerwinski created a subcommittee on welfare reform and appointed me the chairman.

Everyone on the full committee, including Joe, was a member of my subcommittee. This was hot stuff because I was a freshman, and here I was deciding the agenda and chairing the hearings, with Joe sitting beside me. I had the power to take votes and report things out of the committee, just like a real chairman. Some Republican critics pointed out that the Democrats didn't really want to do something about welfare because their only response was a subcommittee with a freshman from liberal Dane County as the chair. They were right on that score, but I was in charge and naive enough to think I could do something.

THE ISSUE OF THE POOR

I knew the basic structure of the welfare programs. I had even written a paper in graduate school on President Richard Nixon's work training program for welfare mothers, and I cared that some people were poor. After all I was a liberal and believed government had an equalizing responsibility. My image of the poor was of the noble immigrant or the African

Americans in the South who were held down by racists. In my military police company in the army, of almost 600 men, only Don Russell ("The Wolfman") from Evansville, Indiana, and I had attended college. The rest were young men of the right age at the wrong time who were caught in the draft because their type had always been cannon fodder. They were African Americans from the South or whites from places like South Philadelphia and South Boston. In my mind they were the poor.

Michael Harrington's *The Other America*, which told of lives of poverty amid plenty, had a profound impact on me, and I was a great believer in Lyndon Johnson's War on Poverty.[1] But I was to learn in my subcommittee that America's welfare programs were having less and less to do with ending poverty, and more and more to do with who the poor were supposed to be and how they were supposed to behave once on welfare.

In America the poor are divided into the deserving and the undeserving. Though both groups are poor because they lack money (obvious, but mostly overlooked as a cause of poverty), welfare programs are reserved for the deserving poor. These are, literally, the children of single mothers.

THE AFDC PROGRAM

The AFDC program (Aid to Families with Dependent Children) began in 1935 as part of the Social Security Act. (Like workmen's compensation and unemployment insurance, social security had its roots with the University of Wisconsin.) Directed toward widows with children, the program was called Aid to Dependent Children (ADC) until the 1960s, when the word "Families" was added. Although semantically this program became broader in scope, and more benevolent in sound, the hook has always been and remains the children. To be eligible for AFDC, you must be a very poor mother of minor children, and you must not be married. A typical AFDC recipient is a nineteen- or twenty-year-old divorced or never married woman with two children under the age of six; she has little work history, she has less than a high school education, and her only asset (the only asset allowed) is an old car. There are some exceptions, and there are other local programs that may be called welfare, but AFDC is the

---

[1] Michael Harrington, *The Other America: Poverty in the United States* (New York: Macmillan, 1962).

battlefield for the "poor wars" that are fought every session in every state legislature.[2]

The federal law on social security requires each state to have an AFDC program, but the federal government pays only about half the cost (based on a formula) and the state pays the rest. In 1993-94 the monthly AFDC grant for a mother with two children ranged widely ($120 in Mississippi, $577 in New York). The program is based on the old-fashioned idea that the poor are locally grown and their community should look after them.

Like a machine that has had new parts added but no old parts discarded, the AFDC program is an outmoded concoction. Food stamps were added as one way to have a national program for the poor that was not restricted by the children-with-single-mother requirement. Thus, all the poor are eligible for food stamps. If you are on AFDC in a state with a small cash grant, you are entitled to more food stamps than if you live in a state with a larger grant. In this way low state grants are supplemented. It is not that Congress thinks poor people in Mississippi need to eat more than the poor in New York. It's a way to give cash from the federal government to the poor without seeming to do so.

The other addition to AFDC was health insurance, called Medicaid, which covers most everything, and there is no deductible or co-payment. AFDC recipients pay nothing out of pocket for this health insurance.

THE LEGISLATIVE LEARNING PROCESS

In my subcommittee we heard testimony about, and debated at length, the small changes in AFDC and Medicaid allowed to the states by federal law. Our Medicaid program was deemed a "Cadillac" program because we included just about all the options allowed. This was not because AFDC recipients had a good lobbyist in Wisconsin. It was because the health care providers in these optional niches were influential. About the only thing the Wisconsin program didn't pay for was chiropractic care. The real pressure was to add coverage for this, not to drop anything that was already covered. (The intense lobbying for and against the idea would even hold the passage of the state budget bill hostage on occasion.)

---

[2] States have the option under the AFDC law to also have an AFDC-Unemployed (AFDC-U) program. Married couples with children may be eligible if they are very poor and the man, the former worker, has exhausted his unemployment benefits. Most states also have a relief program, usually locally funded, that provides temporary help (for example, with food or heating fuel). It may pay some very small weekly or monthly grant for those eligible—mainly young men or single women old enough to have grown children but not old enough for social security.

The subcommittee testimony of university experts, recipients, advocates, and administrators opened my eyes to the seeming futility of trying to reform AFDC's patched together system of programs. AFDC was like prison. It offered security but little chance for escape.

Legislators believe their own staff. They also listen to outside experts who agree with their staff and to anyone from another state. The university types who testified before our subcommittee seemed to have the most influence on AFDC because they knew what had been tried elsewhere and what had failed, and they weren't viewed as partisan. However, for AFDC, a federal law administered by the states, the experts we had to listen to were our own lawyers who spent all of their time telling us all the things we could not do because it wasn't allowed by the federal law.

The program had been changed at the margins with the coming of each new political season. Some years AFDC was defended as a way to allow mothers to stay home with their children. Some years training and work programs and child care provisions were added to help working mothers. Some years these women were blamed for their condition, and some years society was faulted for producing such a culture of dependency. Regardless of whether it was a season when collective charity was offered or a season when individual responsibility was demanded, the status of being poor and staying poor remained constant. Poverty was the required condition if a single mother with children was to get some money, food stamps, and health insurance.

Perhaps the story of white ducks told by my friend Evelyn Owens illustrates the welfare conflict best. She did social work in Dane County for fifty years. The year of the story was 1932:

> One day I was called into the main office. Mr. Hein had a complaint from a member of the county board that I was giving aid to a family who still had 100 white ducks. He demanded to know why. Was it true? Why hadn't I insisted the man divest himself of all assets? Yes, I told him, it was true, but I couldn't understand all the concern. This man had lost his job, was living on the outskirts of the city, and had purchased over 100 little ducks which he planned to raise and sell in the Fall. He told me he could get enough corn and other feed from a farmer relative, and that in the Fall, when he sold them, he would be financially responsible for his family for as long as the money would last.
>
> I told Mr. Hein it seemed so sensible. I couldn't imagine any complaints. In the first place, this family was interested in the ducks! They needed something to do during the long days of unemployment. This plan wasn't costing the county, and I thought it would do something for family morale. Mr. Hein agreed to my arrangement, but I was to explain the situation to the county board member, and not make any more exceptions.[3]

---

[3] From Evelyn Owens's memoir, *Deal the Cards*, privately published in 1991 in Sun Prairie, Wisconsin.

SPECIALIZATION AND EXPERTISE

The subcommittee worked throughout the session and late in the session it issued a report consisting of a list of recommendations, several of which were adopted. By this time I was able to talk about AFDC and the related programs with the air of an expert, and I found I wanted to know more about the issue.

Like students with a declared major, members of a legislature begin to specialize in the issues addressed by the committee or committees on which they serve. Some legislators, usually committee chairs and ranking members, reach a sort of faculty status; other members defer to them and follow their vote on bills in their area. There is an important partisan element to this. When members follow the lead of the expert on their side of the aisle, they must trust that the political problems have been filtered through and that the chosen way to proceed is as politically safe as possible.

I became the expert on child support. It was to me that other Democratic legislators looked for guidance on this complicated issue.

THE GOVERNOR'S COMMISSION

There was an election for governor coming up, and the Democrats were not in very good shape. President Jimmy Carter had tapped Gov. Patrick Lucey to be the ambassador to Mexico, and although his policy victories had left him none too popular, the master was gone. Lt. Gov. Martin Schreiber suddenly became acting governor (a provisional title the Republicans were dutiful in using), and he scrambled to find some things he could point to as his initiatives. Thus, the Welfare Reform Commission was created, and after some lobbying I was named as the only legislative member of the five-member group. (Did anyone else ask?)

Appointing a commission is a time-honored way for governors to buy time, pass the buck, and get out of the line of fire on an issue where action is demanded because of some crisis or the politics of the moment. A group of reasonable citizens with middle-of-the-road credentials is empaneled to study an issue and come up with a proposal that the governor can either implement or shelve. Confined to narrow issues, commissions work well. If the charge is global—to reform taxes or education, for example—the results usually end up on the shelf.

Governor Schreiber's Welfare Reform Commission was a rarity for three reasons: its small size, substantial budget ($200,000), and support personnel (state staff and university experts were assigned to it). The chairman was a professor of economics at the University of Wisconsin, Robert Haveman. His tall good looks and natural smile complemented his idealistic belief that there were economic things—incentives, disincentives, work subsidies—that could be brought to bear in a new way to change the nature of welfare. The chief "expert" was Irv Garfinkel, a twinkly-eyed professor of social work at the University of Wisconsin. He was that dangerous breed of academic liberal who questioned the lore, both liberal and conservative, that had been built up around the programs for the poor since the War on Poverty. He had a powerful idea about child support. He would become more committed to it a little later, when he started to pay child support.

THE CHILD SUPPORT "TAX"

Both Bob and Irv were affiliated with the Institute for Research on Poverty, the original "think tank" for the War on Poverty. Irv had been working on the idea of a child support tax. Upon first hearing the idea, I warned him, "We aren't recommending any tax. Call it something else." Irv's idea was simple: collect child support by withholding from paychecks a set amount. Like the withholding for income taxes, this amount would increase as income went up.

State legislatures often rely on professors at the state university for help. In New Jersey, in a great leap of faith, the legislature even asked a professor from Rutgers to be the swing vote on its reapportionment commission that was equally divided between Republicans and Democrats. An expert from the university is commonly the resource called because, unlike Congress, there is no need or budget for in-house experts in state legislatures.

Irv was our commission's expert and his child support "tax" idea stemmed from two things. First, AFDC was literally money from the federal government to support children who were not being supported by their parents. It was child support. Second, the method of collecting and disbursing child support was a disaster. Under Wisconsin state law, child support was something that was negotiated as part of a divorce settlement; the level of financial support was a portion of the income that was left after the father's personal expenses—rent, car, and so on— were handled. Often child support was bargained away in the haggle between the lawyers for the two sides, with the mother giving it up to avoid the custody fight threatened by the father. The judge would then ratify this peace treaty as if it were some dime-on-a-dollar resolution of bankruptcy.

If there was a child support *award*, the word implying exactly what it means—support "won" and ordered by the judge—the noncustodial parent, the father in 90 percent of the cases, was expected to pay the amount each month to the local county clerk, who would in turn then pass it on to the mother. It did not matter if the amount was enough money to actually support the children. If the money was late in coming or not paid at all, the enforcement mechanism was to go back to court and have the judge threaten the father with contempt—a cumbersome, inefficient, and costly process.

POLICY ANALYSIS

The commission shaped Irv's idea into a plan. Along the way some sacred cows were culled from the big herd that hung around child support and AFDC. The first cow died when we learned the child support system was a fraud. Children were being knowingly swindled by adults. It turned out that child support orders existed for only about half of all eligible children, and only half of this group received any money. In most cases it was not the full amount and it was late in coming. The "system" was one big lie to children, and it was not some benign fib like Santa Claus; it was a thing that hurt.

Nonpayment of child support, inadequate payment, or irregular payment were the major causes of AFDC dependency. It was taken for granted that child support was not being paid to AFDC mothers because the fathers couldn't afford it or were on the lam. Irv had compared the income of fathers in AFDC cases with child support awards and the income of fathers in AFDC cases without awards, and he had found that there was little difference in income. It was not the case that some could pay and did, and some could not pay and did not. It was just random, like luck.

It was taken for granted that judges, lawyers, and county clerks must support the current system of child support. As it turned out, divorce lawyers deplored the necessity of using the children as pawns in order to win their clients' cases. Judges knew the system didn't work, especially the idea that they could actually enforce the payment of child support. Judges knew that every day the system called for them to sentence women and children to welfare. And clerks felt no responsibility and wondered why shuffling the checks of the formerly married was their job. Was it because they issued marriage licenses in the first place?

It was not taken for granted that child support was an intrinsic good and a responsibility of parents. I could detect no social stigma attached to those, rich or poor, who did not pay the child support they legally owed. Advocates for welfare recipients argued against pursuing child support, suggesting it should not be expected from those who they assumed were poor themselves. Some fathers' groups argued that support should not be paid unless there was some accounting to prove the children (not the ex-wife) received the money. Other fathers argued that it was right to withhold support if they felt they were wronged in the divorce settlement, or the custody arrangement was unfair and not enforced by the court, or visitation was denied. The withholding of child support was also a way a father could protest the judge's "rule of nurture" that assumed mothers always were given custody.

Under the law child support was supposed to be collected in AFDC cases. However, this was to defray the cost of the grant and made no difference in the amount of money received by the mother or children. It was taken for granted that working was better than not working. However, the law required working mothers receiving AFDC money to give almost all of their earned income to the state to defray the cost of the AFDC grant.

Finally, the commission considered the public's stereotypical views of welfare recipients. They were thought to be either conniving welfare queens with Cadillacs, or women who were victims and down on their luck. The truth was that every case was unique. Nevertheless, AFDC treated them all the same.

PUTTING A PLAN TOGETHER

Irv's idea evolved throughout the Welfare Reform Commission's discovery process and formed the centerpiece of its recommendations, which would become the welfare reform plan the governor would present to the legislature. We recommended that the question of child support awards be completely removed from the courts and that the former system be replaced by a legal presumption that children would have a right to child support in all cases. The amount of child support awarded and the method of collection would also be radically changed. Child support would be withheld by employers from paychecks, like taxes, and it would be a percentage of the *gross* income of the noncustodial parent. Based on more of Irv's research, we pegged child support at 17 percent of gross income for one child, 23 percent for two children, and so on. Thus, if gross income was $100,000, child support for one child would be $17,000. If gross income were $10,000, child support would be $1,700.[4]

---

[4] The amount was 17 percent of gross income for one child; 23, 29, 31, and 34 percent respectively for two, three, four, and five or more children.

This was no longer the "bread and water and a little more" concept of traditional child support. The plan gave children a new right and ensured collection and adequacy of support. It was income sharing. "The purpose of the change," we proclaimed with all the bravado of musketeers, was to "articulate in law a clear societal expectation in cases of divorce, separation, and paternity that children are entitled to something approximating the standard of living which they would have enjoyed had the family remained intact." [5]

If the kid went skiing in Switzerland before the divorce, he or she should be able to schuss in New Hampshire after the divorce. And regardless of how little parental income there was, some of it, even if just a token, must be shared with the child. At no point would parents' financial responsibility for their own children be excused. Irv and I could not rationalize excusing rich or poor fathers from the obligation to share income with their own children. Fathers who live with their children share their income with them, whether a little or a lot, so why excuse fathers who live apart from their children?

THE INFLUENCE OF VALUES

As Progressives had done in years past, experts from the University of Wisconsin joined with the state government to devise a new policy that addressed an old problem. The policy reflected how the commission wanted the world to be and how it felt people should behave. I wanted parents to be like my parents, and I wanted children to have a childhood like mine. Beaver Cleaver should be the norm. The idea of withholding child support from wages had the tax element and efficiency that economists like, but it also had much to do with Irv's frustrating experience in trying to pay his own child support. He had wanted the payroll people at the university to take his payment from his paycheck and automatically send it along to the clerk, something they would do if they received a directive from the clerk. However, the clerk could not do this in Irv's case because he wasn't delinquent in making his payments. Irv could see firsthand that the clerk's office was not going to be the crucible for reform in the future.

Our proposed changes went far beyond AFDC. They affected everyone—kids, parents, courts, and clerks. The policy horizon lay far before us, and a knowing wind seemed to push us on. In our final recommenda-

---

[5] Preface to the *Wisconsin Welfare Reform Study, 1978: Report and Recommendations of the Welfare Reform Study Advisory Committee.*

tion we said, in effect, "Assume the new income sharing, withholding, percentage-of-income plan was in place and working. Let's now throw out the AFDC concept and replace it with an assured child support payment." The child support "tax" was Irv's idea. The "assured benefit" was his dream.

An assured benefit would be a guaranteed minimum income floor under each child. A mother could add child support and wages, plus a wage supplement for child care, to this floor, without penalty, until a target income that was above the poverty level was reached. Child support payments would not be penalized (that is, the money would not be used to defray the cost of the grant), and work would become an economically rational act because wages could be kept. The assured benefit would be open to all single mothers, not just those on AFDC.

THE PERSONAL DIMENSION

I spent from 1977 to 1989 trying to get the Wisconsin legislature to enact the new child support system and the assured benefit. In addition to the long legislative process, there was a personal journey that shaped my views and held me constant in my persistence.

First, I became convinced that children should have the legal right to financial support from their parents. In the bargaining process of divorce, a child's financial needs were on the list of the parents' financial obligations, somewhere below rent but perhaps above the plumber's bill. I felt it was my responsibility, as a person in a position of power, to right this wrong.

Second, I became a father. Alec, the first of our two children, was born about 3:00 A.M. on the clear morning of June 19, 1981. There is no poet or philosopher that I can quote here to express the feeling of love I immediately felt for this little baby. He was immortality. I remember one moment during his infancy with the clarity of a color snapshot. I was bathing him in the sink in the bathroom that is off our bedroom. The sink is pale white, and the counter is dull red. A mirror spans the width of the room but stops before it reaches the ceiling to accommodate a row of light bulbs, like those in a backstage dressing room. In the mirror I watched the two of us as if I were not the one in the reflection. I envisioned taking a bullet in the chest or diving in front of a car in order to save Alec and show him my love because no words existed to express such feelings. Perhaps I became the legislature's Pied Piper for children on this day.

THE PROCESS CONTINUES

When Governor Schreiber was defeated and Republican maverick Lee Sherman Dreyfus took office, the Welfare Reform Commission's report could have been orphaned. Fortunately, the new governor kept Donald Percy, the capable secretary of the Department of Health and Social Services who had promoted and protected the commission. He made sure the recommendations would not die just because there was a new administration. However, there was now no one to promote the recommendations with the legislature except me. Therefore, like an elected prophet in possession of the revealed truth, I set about making converts.

Enacting the child support withholding system into law took ten years. Then I worked two more years on a child support assurance bill, only to see it vetoed by Gov. Tommy Thompson. During this long journey, I was aided by allies, like Irv, who stayed the whole course, and becoming Speaker certainly helped. Indeed, it is very unlikely that the child support withholding law would have happened in Wisconsin if I had not been the Speaker because it was necessary to have the power to arrange things in advance, much like one needs to secure a site, order lumber, and hire carpenters in order to build a house. The blueprint alone will not do it.

A STUDY LEADS TO A LAW

If a member can get a legislature to study an issue (other than abortion!), the legislature usually will pass a bill that embodies most of the study committee's recommendations. In the Wisconsin legislature the best forum for studying an issue was the Legislative Council, which was the legal staff for the regular standing committees as well as the research staff for the Legislative Council's study committees. In the period between sessions (from June to January of election years), these study committees would take a vexing problem, study it, find a consensus, and then prepare a bill.

Every legislature has some organization like Wisconsin's Legislative Council. The council refers to two things: the committee of leaders from both parties and both houses that decides on subjects for study, and the lawyers and researchers who staff the study committees. The committees are unique because experts, advocates, lobbyists, and ordinary citizens make up about half of the study committee membership and thus have a direct hand in drafting a bill that is more than likely to become law.

Almost without exception, legislative leaders will introduce a "Legislative Council bill." It comes into the regular legislative process with an imprimatur that says to the other members, "This bill is OK. It's a Leg Council bill." When I became the Speaker I chaired the Council every other session, switching with the Senate leader. As chairman, I had a great deal to say about what issues would be on the council's study list; and one study I could pick as my own. Through this study-to-law method I was able, over the years, to move through the system a tax break for the working poor (the Earned Income Tax Credit) and other parts of the Welfare Reform Commission's recommendations.

When I first introduced the Welfare Reform Commission's plan as a bill in the 1979 session, I was only in my second term, not yet in the leadership, and Republican governor Dreyfus was in office, so the bill went nowhere. Yet I made some progress. I was able to add an amendment to the budget bill that required delinquent child support to be withheld from state income tax refunds.

A former Wisconsin legislator living in Florida had sent me a clipping that mentioned the idea. After two frustrating years of listening to reasons why things could not be done to change the state's child support system, I immediately latched on to the new idea. Introducing the amendment was like throwing an apple to a pig. The amendment came, and the members were startled; after turning it all around and finding no way to oppose it, indeed realizing it to be a juicy political find, they let it be adopted.

NEW SPEAKER, NEW GOVERNOR

Governor Dreyfus did not run for reelection. The new governor was my friend Tony Earl, and I was the new Speaker. This made it quite easy to start the child support idea in the new governor's first budget. I had supported him in the primary, and he was not about to deny me my child support experiment.

Legislative leaders, by necessity, huddle often with the governor on legislative issues. The governor wants something on his or her agenda to pass; the leaders tell the governor the political problems with the initiative and suggest another way to approach the issue. Or the leaders want something, and the governor has problems. Tony and I were in the best position for cooperation to get something done. We were of the same party, we were newly elected, we wanted to establish a good record, and, most importantly, we were friends. We could talk without thinking the other had a hidden agenda.

In fairly short order the child support withholding language was added to the budget bill. To the casual reader the language appeared to authorize a demonstration or pilot project the state would try in one or more counties. The Department of Health and Social Services was directed to enter into contracts with up to ten counties to withhold child support from wages in new cases of divorce, separation, or paternity. The department was then asked to publish a child support standard based on a percentage of the noncustodial parent's income. Judges could use this standard to determine support.

The problem was that we did not want our program to be a pilot. If it were just a test of the idea, we probably would get in legal trouble by treating some cases differently than others. Furthermore, I did not want to come back in another session and try to win support for our idea again, which would be required if the program started as a pilot. As a result, we fine-tuned the budget language. The withholding of tax refunds from noncustodial parents would be restricted initially to a maximum of ten counties. Within five years, however, all counties would be required to adopt income withholding in all new cases. This language, combined with the separate language requiring the department to write the percentage rules, had the effect of making the whole scheme state law in five years.

BUILDING SUPPORT

Child support seemed on the fast track in the legislature, until an enthusiastic family court judge in Racine County volunteered to be the first one to try out the system. We did not know that Racine had a very large and vocal fathers' rights group that was mad about support, custody, and visitation. (Many feared that all existing arrangements governing child support would be altered.) This county should have been the last place to implement our scheme, and only then after it had been on the road and had been polished. It was definitely not the best place to try to start. Everyone in the county was in an uproar by the time Irv and I were invited down to explain the fairness of our supposedly brilliant plan.

It seemed odd that this informational meeting was held at J.I. Case High School until we walked into the gym and immediately realized that we were the opposing team and this was a home game. The bright game lights were on, and the bleachers were filled with more than five hundred people. Most of them were divorced dads who were there with their second or, in more than a few cases, third wives. They had not come to listen to what might happen to people who got divorced in the future. They were there to tell us, in no uncertain terms, that they were mad. Divorce was bad enough, but the legal decisions they had to live with concerning child support, custody, and visitation were hell. The system was unfair, punitive, and arbitrary.

Irv and I took turns speaking our piece, standing behind a podium and facing the crowd from across the basketball floor. We did our best, and Irv became absolutely invigorated each time he was on the court. He would come back to sit next to me looking like he had just held the star player on the other side to two points. From experience I knew to hold to my position because the crowd had no votes in the legislature or my district, and there would be other battles on other days. I might have seemed unsympathetic to the fathers because after the meeting the sheriff, who was there with a deputy, thought it best to walk me to my car at the far end of the parking lot. "I don't think this is necessary," I protested. He replied in a soft voice, "I think it is." The sheriff, a divorced man himself, had recognized quite a few off-duty policemen and deputies in the crowd, all armed with their revolvers, and he decided that it would not help his career if the Speaker were winged in his county.

A MORE ENLIGHTENED STRATEGY

I had built up a pretty good disgust at fathers who did not support their children. Many a time I had said in public that welfare was caused by men who did not support their children, and I had pondered in the press whether we shouldn't have a law that would place the father officially on welfare so he could enjoy some of the stigma suffered by his children. The meeting in Racine made Irv and me realize some things that helped guide our strategy from that point on.

First, if this plan was going to work, it needed local political support. Therefore, we decided that the Department of Health and Social Services should "require" the county board to vote to be one of the ten initial counties withholding refunds. This requirement had the psychological effect of making participation in the project feel like a contest where the first ten, but only the first ten, entrants would win. The idea was to make our product more dear and have the local judge and the social workers sell it to the local politicians. We now realized our plan needed to start out in the small counties before it hit the Broadway of the big troubled counties. The board vote requirement, which could be lobbied through quickly in smaller counties, would tend to accomplish this.

Second, I set up an "implementation advisory committee" and appointed as members all the critics of the withholding plan I could find. The judges were represented. Lawyers who did divorce work were represented. The employers, who would have to do the paperwork for the withholding, had a member. (We ended up allowing employers to keep a dollar per transaction for their cost.) And the head of the father's group in Racine, a city cop, was appointed, which was brilliant because he ended up an enthusiastic supporter of the idea.

Third, I got my head on a little straighter about things when Dane County judge Dan Moeser said to me one day, "Tom, the trouble with the current system is that too many fathers leave the courtroom thinking the law has taken their children away, that they are no longer a father like other fathers. Don't do anything to promote this; it's the worst thing that could happen." Indeed, child support was not an isolated issue in divorce, as the following comments in Racine had shown me. "Why pay support when we can't see the kids?" one father asked. Another complained: "She doesn't spend the money on the kids. They come to my house in old clothes, and I have to buy them decent things." Still another asked this question: "How can we pay support when the support my wife has coming from her ex-husband doesn't arrive?" As Irv often said, "It's unlikely people who can't get along in marriage will be friends after the divorce Tom. That's why we are doing this."

THE FEDERAL FACTOR

After Racine we took pains to make each step toward statewide implementation one where we consulted everyone who could be a stumbling block. Once we felt the home front well in control, we sought approval from the federal government to enact the assured benefit in Wisconsin. We needed a waiver because the AFDC law didn't allow such experimentation.

The states implement and administer national laws dealing with health care for the poor, air and water pollution, transportation, and welfare. The states get paid to act as agents of the federal government in this way, and they have a little leeway—very little—in how they go about it. It is hard to get a waiver.

I enlisted the help of the lobbying arm of the National Conference of State Legislatures in Washington, D.C. Our child support initiative was a rare chance for the conference to help one state without harming another. Usually it could do little because a broad consensus was lacking. (On what issue do all fifty states agree?) But in this case the change would only affect one state, Wisconsin. Then we had a bit of luck and made a right strategy decision. The luck was that the capable David Reimer, a former aide to Governor Lucey, happened to be on the NCSL staff, and he was assigned to the task. The right decision turned out to be asking Congress for a law specifically giving Wisconsin this waiver. This was a much wiser course of action than trying to convince the federal Department of Health and Human Services to give this one state an administrative waiver.

At this time President Ronald Reagan was promoting his "New Federalism," an initiative intended to sort out the responsibilities of the states and the federal government. Reagan had proposed that the states take over welfare and that the federal government take over health care. Although this particular idea was dead on arrival in Congress, the mood was in favor of giving the states more responsibility for these programs. (The pendulum was swinging back toward the notion that the poor were local.) Our timing couldn't have been better. Not only was the attitude right, but there was a child support bill moving through Congress that had broad support. We saw this bill as a handy vehicle to hook our waiver on as a rider.

David Reimer and the people in the Wisconsin office in Washington, D.C., bombarded the right committee in the Democratically controlled House and the right committee in the Republican controlled Senate with information about Wisconsin's child support plan. I worked on the Wisconsin delegation, especially the Democrats, who could hardly be against this waiver for their own state, and they found it easy to ask their colleagues to throw them this bone not asked for by any other state.

At each step we had to explain the assured benefit, and each person who heard the idea liked the idea. Some of the conservatives squirmed a bit because they thought the idea sounded too much like a scheme for a guaranteed income, but they could hardly be against allowing a state its right, shall we say, to experiment with the poor. Some of the liberals in the U.S. Congress thought this idea was OK for a progressive state like Wisconsin to try; they wondered, however, if it would mean they would have to grant something else, not so enlightened, for Mississippi? We overcame all this, and the bill with the waiver attached as an amendment passed the House. In the Senate, however, our little amendment became the center of controversy. The secretary of the Department of Health and Human Services, Margaret Heckler, decided to fight the waiver because it was being granted by Congress rather than her department.

We had our showdown with the administration the day of the hearing on the bill before the Senate Finance Committee. I appeared to make the case for the waiver, and Secretary Heckler appeared to ask that the Wisconsin language be removed. God bless Sen. Bob Dole, the chairman, and Sen. Russell Long, the ranking minority member. These two legislative foxes understood what we were up to, and they didn't take kindly to the notion that the administration wanted states to experiment but didn't think Congress should have any part in granting the permission. Personally, I thought this administration believed in states' rights about as much as George III.

Some weeks after the Senate action, Irv and I, seated in the ballroom of the Washington Sheraton Hotel, watched as President Reagan signed the child support bill. It had passed the Congress unanimously, and it contained, tucked away in a back-page paragraph, our dream language allowing Wisconsin to experiment with an assured benefit. We thought Wisconsin was going to lead again.

The child support law, after the first few counties signed on, gained rather quick acceptance, and if a glitch came up, Irv and I would work to fix it and smooth the way toward the day that Milwaukee County would opt in. Almost half of the AFDC caseload in the state was in the city of Milwaukee. The sheer number of child support cases there could ruin the reputation of the new system if the bugs were not worked out first in the smaller counties. The worst thing that could happen would be for a county to have a bad experience and complain to its representatives in the legislature. This would bring unwanted attention to the phase-in plan, which was progressing smoothly but could still be stopped.

I wanted to remain the Speaker long enough to see this law safely in place and to implement the federal waiver, which gave Wisconsin ten years to test the assured benefit. Also, a new and very disturbing trend had come to light.

THE NEW ISSUE: PATERNITY

The information that more than 20 percent of the births in Wisconsin each year were out of wedlock was not known to Irv and me until years into our effort to change the child support laws and well after the end of the Welfare Reform Commission. We were both shocked. This statistic seemed amazingly high. Then we learned that in most other states the percentage was higher and growing everywhere. For minorities, out-of-wedlock births were the norm. For African Americans in the state the rate was over 50 percent and skyrocketing. (By 1992 the Wisconsin rate had grown to 26.1 percent of all births and 82 percent of all African-American births.)[6] What chance was there for child support, regardless of the system, when a big slice of a whole generation of kids was missing legal paternity? Under the law a father has no financial obligation for a child unless paternity has been established.

The paternity statistics came out, by chance, during a Legislative Council study committee on health insurance for the uninsured that I was chairing. We also learned that only half the children born out of wedlock would ever see paternity established, and this figure included all adop-

---

[6] Wisconsin Department of Health and Social Services, Division of Health, Center for Health Statistics.

tions. The committee recommended that the state pursue paternity for any child whose birth certificate did not include a father's name. Also recommended was a new "affidavit of paternity" form to be presented to nonmarried parents before they left the hospital.

It turned out that Wisconsin law prohibited a father from putting his name on his child's birth certificate unless he was married to the child's mother. Biology to the contrary, these fathers of the blank-birth-certificate children did not have the status of legal fathers unless they went to court and, more or less, petitioned to be the dad.

Many new fathers, perhaps the majority, were not evading paternity. They just gave up on the legal hassle of claiming paternity, especially after leaving the hospital, the place where almost all parents complete the birth certificate paperwork. This illegitimacy of unmarried fathers, which probably originated when a bastard in Britain claimed to be the son of a lord, made being a father optional for many and created a growing class of children who had no right to a legal father.

The affidavit idea stemmed from our experience with naming Alec. The nurse was responsible for getting the parents to fill out the birth certificate, which would be filed with the state by the hospital, and she wasn't going to let us head for the exit without choosing a name to put on the certificate. I remembered the psychology of this and felt that if a new state law required the hospital to present a paternity affidavit to daddy to sign before mom and the baby left the hospital, a new way to establish paternity would start to take hold in the case of unmarried parents.

Once again a study committee quickly led to a law. The Legislative Council recommended two significant changes in Wisconsin laws governing paternity. First, it allowed unmarried fathers to sign an affidavit stating that they were the father; the affidavit was then filed with the birth certificate of their children. In this way paternity was presumed under the law. Second, it required the state to pursue paternity if there was not a man's name on the birth certificate. A paternity bill containing both elements was passed that very session by the legislature. I sincerely hoped that this beachhead in the law would one day cause a judge to declare that every child had a constitutional right to a father. This was part of my unrealistic belief that all children should have a childhood like mine.

A CHANGE IN ADMINISTRATION

The chances were good that progress on child support and paternity would continue apace. The Democrats were in control of both houses of the legislature, Democratic governor Earl was in the East Wing, and the

Republicans didn't seem likely to take over either house or, given their meager stable of potential candidates, defeat Tony Earl. What could go wrong?

The gracious and honest Tony Earl, whose crime was believing that good government was good politics, regardless of how it was prepared or served, was defeated by conservative Tommy Thompson, the Assembly's minority leader. Tommy hadn't looked formidable, but the Democrats had been lulled into thinking Wisconsin was now a liberal state. They wrongly thought Earl's considerable political troubles would be offset by the advantages of incumbency.

There is a cache of wine in the basement of the governor's mansion, and there is one bottle designated for each governor to consume before he or she leaves office. One winter night after Tony had been defeated for reelection, Senate Majority Leader Tim Cullen, Tony, and I gathered for dinner in the governor's mansion with our wives. We drank Tony's bottle of red wine and talked of things done and things left undone. I did not know that one thing left undone—more accurately, unsent—was the letter that executed the contract between Wisconsin and the federal government detailing how the assured benefit would be implemented. Congress had granted the waiver, but Margaret Heckler's department was making us go through a lot of hoops before it signed off on the experiment. This letter represented the final dotting of i's and crossing of t's that it had demanded.

The letter wasn't sent because Tony, and Linda Reivitz, his secretary of health and social services, thought it proper that the incoming administration be given a chance to review the agreement first. Had this letter been sent, rather than left to the unfriendly hands of the new administration, my bargaining position with the new administration would not have been so weak and perhaps the assured benefit would have had its test drive.

Fortunately, Governor Thompson appointed a Democrat, my friend and colleague Tim Cullen, to be the new secretary of the Department of Health and Social Services. Although the assured benefit test, and the agreement with the federal government that included the design of the test, had to be worked out again with the new administration, I would have a friend in charge of the negotiations on this part of the upcoming state budget.

COLLECTIVE LEADERSHIP

Thompson had campaigned on the idea of cutting welfare benefits by 5 percent and using the savings for work training. This seductive idea hit every hot button voters had about welfare, but it was something that the

Democrats in the legislature were not about to do. He also wanted to reduce AFDC benefits for women whose children did not show up at school—his so-called "learnfare" initiative.

There is a general rule that a governor, especially a new governor, gets most of what he or she wants, and a Speaker and Senate leader get some of the things they feel strongly about. This expectation of outcome, like oil in an engine, is what moves things along until the final pieces of an important bill, like the state budget bill, are put in place. So the governor knew, and I knew, and Tim Cullen knew, and Joe Strohl (the new Senate majority leader) knew that the legislature would pass some sort of welfare reform package. Not wanting too many cooks to spoil the broth, we decided to each add an ingredient and in the end pronounce it stew. In this way we would make a dish to pass.

In the negotiations I agreed to support a version of learnfare, restricting it to teen mothers who would be aided in getting a high school degree, and Tommy agreed to the language needed to move the assured benefit to the next step, which was the federal agreement and permission for Secretary Cullen to try to find a pilot county. Actually, it meant Irv and I would work to find a county because after our Racine experience we knew, like realtors, that location was everything. Thus we arranged for Dane County to be the volunteer. Democratic county executive Rick Phelps, who was a friend and owed me more than a few favors, agreed to test the plan. He understood it and could see that it would mean he could legitimately claim to be fostering reform of welfare. Then we needed a smaller control county to volunteer. With some help from the local legislator, we found Shawano County, which was small but had a considerable AFDC population and a willing administrator.

Unfortunately, the assured benefit never made it. Tim Cullen left the Thompson administration after eighteen months, and Dane County decided it could not test the assured benefit without some more money from the state, and Tommy Thompson realized that I was going to run for governor against him. That was the end of the assured benefit. I was able to get the money Dane County wanted (a measly $80,000) to the governor's desk twice, but he vetoed it both times.

POLITICAL RIVALRIES

If you are a politician, your potential opponents command a special spot in your brain, and you find yourself involuntarily concentrating on what "they" are doing. It's a natural thing like putting your tongue on a bad tooth. For example, in reapportionment battles I saw many incumbents pursue district changes designed to exclude someone they had heard third-hand was thinking about running against them, even if this meant that they picked up areas that had a history of voting for the other party.

I certainly thought about Governor Thompson, and he certainly thought about me, as we approached the race for governor in 1990. The assured benefit became a victim of the upcoming campaign. The plan was well understood within the administration. The numbers had been crunched for cost, and many inside the bureaucracy were promoting it, pointing out that only Wisconsin had this waiver. And it would not have been any real problem for the governor to rather quickly take credit for the innovation. Governors own what they sign, so who got credit could be manipulated—if it turned out to be something that worked as well as the theory promised. However, if it did work, it might be worse than if it did not work. Here hangs the tale, for it was welfare that killed the assured benefit.

When the numbers were crunched, it became clear that many women would leave AFDC because their incomes would increase, making them ineligible. However, the problem was the new big group of single women with children who would become eligible for the assured benefit—those not quite poor enough for AFDC or too proud for welfare. What would they be "on"? Would it look like a whole new bunch of welfare mothers was being created, regardless of the fact that it was a small stipend, less than AFDC, that rewarded work and child support? If the government, in effect, replaced the dole by supplementing wages and child support, wouldn't you risk the public, the voters, coming to think this was the "new" welfare? In the end the vetoes came not because of political rivalries or the risk of the wrong politician getting the credit. The assured benefit died this time because welfare is comfortable—the lines are drawn, the rhetoric is in place—and change is risky. Someone should be on welfare or off welfare. That's the safe debate. Social security is for old people, not children.

ARKANSAS EPILOGUE

In 1987 Gov. Bill Clinton came to Wisconsin to speak at the Democratic Party Convention in Stevens Point. He knew of my work on child support, and we sat down in his hotel room and talked for about an hour about child support wage withholding and the assured benefit. He knew his stuff. A presidential election was looming for the Democrats, and we talked of the new ideas it would take for a return to the White House.

I had arranged for a dozen or so state legislators and staffers who monkeyed with presidential politics to drop by to meet him after our chat. Six of the seven presidential candidates who would run in the 1988 Democratic primary in Wisconsin came to Stevens Point and spoke. But it was Bill Clinton, the dinner speaker, who was not running, who stole the show. He may have won the Wisconsin primary in April 1992 because of that impressive speech to the liberals in the audience who had not known a thing about him before that night.

As chairman of Michael Dukakis's presidential campaign in Wisconsin, I became one of many people who suggested that Bill Clinton give the keynote address at the Democratic Convention in Atlanta. We called the Dukakis people and the chair of the Democratic Party to testify that this guy could give a good speech with a message the Democrats could take to the bank. He was chosen to give the less prestigious nominating speech. He would be addressing a prime-time national audience, and just minutes before he spoke I stopped in the waiting room to wish him well. I was thinking to myself that this is a cinch, a star is born, and I had already set it up that he would come to the Wisconsin delegation's breakfast meeting the next morning to be triumphant. I could picture the smiley scene and the press clippings in the Wisconsin papers that would surely follow.

Well, the speech was disastrous, much too long and complicated, and he was actually booed by some delegates. The Arkansas delegation sat behind us, and after the speech Clinton returned to his seat on the aisle next to Hillary. I told my aide, Stephanie Case, whom Clinton did not know, to go back to tell him it was a good speech. She said, "What! That speech was horrible." She went anyway. And the next morning he came to our breakfast caucus, and there were press clippings in the Wisconsin papers—quite a few.

The moral to this story is that we became friends, and I ended up chairing the Clinton campaign in 1992 in Wisconsin. As president, he championed the idea—Irv's idea—of an assured benefit.

9

The Teachers' Union:
Influence Where It Counts

In almost every state legislature the teachers' union is the most powerful interest group. Teachers are spread out around a state much like legislators—according to population. Each legislative district has close to the same number of people in it. This means that there will be a similar number of school age kids in each district, and this means there will be close to the same number of public school teachers in each district. This even distribution, along with teachers' tight organization and sophisticated campaign techniques, brings a natural political clout.

The focus of any teachers' union is the state legislature, which controls the money to fund public education and has sole authority over teachers' bread-and-butter issues, such as pensions. Perhaps most important, the legislature is the place where bad things can be stopped from happening, and it only takes a majority of one house to say no.

This chapter explains how this powerful interest group is organized for maximum political influence in lobbying and elections. Through independent expenditure campaigns, the teachers' union skillfully uses money, polls, focus groups, and phone banks to help elect its friends and defeat the not so friendly.

THE RISE TO POWER

If castle architecture had evolved, the modern incarnation of the art would be the Wisconsin teachers' union building atop Nob Hill on the south side of Madison. From the bank of ten-foot-high windows in the board room of this new, postfortress structure, the view to the North across Lake Monona is striking. There, rising from the isthmus between the lakes and dead in the center of town, you can see the state capitol, a classic four-winged beauty of a building constructed with granite and marble. On its dome, rising 284 feet from the floor, is a statue of a woman clad in gold leaf with a badger on her head and a globe in her hand. She symbolizes the state motto: "Forward." It is appropriate that the view from the teachers' union headquarters focuses on the state capitol building. That is where the legislature is.

The rise to power of teachers' unions started with their fight to gain collective bargaining rights. Morris Andrews, the former head of the Wisconsin teachers' union and its lobbyist from 1972 until 1992, was the teachers' general in the collective bargaining war in Wisconsin.

In 1965 "Morrie" was a government teacher and a football coach ("fifth best record in school history") at Big Rapids High School in western Michigan. The school board had given the bank president's son (a student at Big Rapids) an academic award that the teachers felt was undeserved. To protest they mounted a write in campaign for a challenger in the school board election and came close to toppling an incumbent. This political activism by the local teachers was rare. Public school teachers usually stayed out of school board elections. The community became really upset when the teachers caused a recall election of board members over a principal chosen by the board, a former colleague they knew was unqualified.

Morrie was the spokesman for the teachers in both electoral battles. Because Michigan's governor, George Romney, had just signed a bill legalizing collective bargaining by teachers, the next logical step was to bring in help from the Michigan Education Association, the state union. The state people could recognize organizing talent, mostly because they saw it so rarely, and soon Morrie was working for the union. There was a lot of work because the new law meant teachers had to be trained how to bargain with their school board. Next in Morrie's career came a stint as the field director for the Illinois teachers' union and a year with the national union training negotiators around the country. In 1972 he came to Wisconsin to be the executive director of the Wisconsin Education Association Council, always called "WEAC" and pronounced as a cuss word by its political rivals.

Patton became a general when he was needed—when there was a war—and Morrie became head of WEAC just as a teachers' strike over salary in the tiny town of Hortonville set off a no-holds-barred battle in the state over the pay levels and rights of teachers. A teachers' strike divides a small town like a railroad track. You are either on the right side or the wrong side, and it's that way forever.

Under Morrie's direction, WEAC organized meetings in support of the Hortonville teachers in every school district in the state. As a result of those emotional gatherings, the Wisconsin Education Association was reborn as a teachers' "union." WEAC also raised enough money in those meetings to pay the salaries of the striking Hortonville teachers for a year. After Hortonville, WEAC turned its attention to the legislature, and the effort to gain a collective bargaining bill specifically for teachers began in earnest. It was then that most legislators and candidates discovered the teachers' union was also in their home town.

Morrie has a kind yet wily face, like Droopy the dog in the cartoons, and he doesn't wear ties. It was not his personal clout, or personal relationships, that made him powerful. It was the aura of WEAC and its presence in every legislative district. Morrie embodied this power and carried it like a big gun concealed under a tight coat.

The teachers' union would win the bargaining bill because teachers are in every community. They have leverage where it counts, and they have a limited agenda. This lends itself to a most effective organizational structure. Education also has a special place in America and, to state the really obvious, every politician was once a student.

APPORTIONED FOR POLITICAL POWER

Teachers are influential in legislative races because they come already apportioned for political power. As noted earlier, there are roughly the same number of teachers in every legislative district. The AFL-CIO, trial lawyers, chiropractors, doctors, the brewery workers, farmers, bankers, dog track investors, and anti-abortion activists, along with a lot of other interest groups, are players in legislative races and politics. On election day, however, they can deliver votes only in the legislative districts where they are located. Only the teachers are in every candidate's home town.

Teachers' electoral influence tends to be the greatest in rural and suburban areas, where teachers often are the biggest and best-organized fish in the political pond. As a result, teachers have a disproportionate influence in the marginal seats. The marginal seats (seats that can be won by either party) are relatively few in number, but they are always located, by definition, where neither party is dominant. Democrats are strong in cities, and Republicans are strong in suburbs. Elsewhere the teachers' union can tip the balance.

This power to influence the outcome of marginal races means the teachers' union has a lot to say about which party controls the legislature. Moreover, the union endorses candidates running in the primaries of both parties. It is therefore not written off by the Republicans as a Democratic union that is forever with the other side. The union has a lot of influence with legislators of both parties in the marginal seats, and this means clout on the close votes when the issue is one that really matters to the union. It is power at the legislature's fulcrum.

ORGANIZATIONAL STRUCTURE

Although WEAC's organizational chart looks like the typical corporate pyramid, it is really the bottom layer that has the power. In each school district the teachers and others in the union, like the hot-lunch cooks and bus drivers, are structured into a bargaining unit and choose a political committee. These units are then grouped by region where they employ a staff to work on campaigns. The local teachers hire and direct this staff, not the big shots in the WEAC castle in Madison. A policymaking assembly and a state board of directors also are chosen at the regional level. The board elects the WEAC president, who must be an active teacher, and it appoints the executive director of WEAC. Everyone elected has term limits so turnover is assured, and presumably factions do not develop. The structure gives ownership and a sense of control to the local teachers.

The endorsement process also contributes to the union's power because it, too, is controlled locally. The candidate for the legislature first meets WEAC when he or she receives an invitation to an "endorsement interview." This interview is usually an anxious affair for the first-time candidate—not only because of the union's mystique but also because of the inevitable sighting of a former teacher, or perhaps a child's current teacher, among the dozen or so recognizable faces gathered for the inquiry. Every candidate in the state is asked the same questions, but it is the hometown teachers doing the asking and making the recommendation, which is then mailed to all the other union members in the candidate's legislative district for final ratification. It is this latter step that also sets the teachers apart. In the AFL-CIO process, which is quite typical, the local union leaders decide on the endorsement, but there is no ratification by the rank and file.

For the incumbent legislator running for reelection, the WEAC endorsement process is not restricted to the campaign period. Incumbents who voted with the union 80 percent or more of the time in a legislative session are automatically endorsed for reelection. The roll call of votes is assembled at the end of the session, but it is apparent during the session which votes WEAC is likely to use. Of course, a legislator will think hard about the wisdom of voting against the WEAC position. This endorsement process made enough waves in the voting behavior of the members that it became part of the rhythm of each session. It often caused the leadership to ponder whether to bring up certain bills for a vote that might cause trouble for members vis-à-vis the WEAC roll call. (On the other hand, occasionally we would seek votes on bills that Democrats could easily support but Republicans could not.)

Members suspected that the Speaker had a hand in choosing the votes for the WEAC roll call, and I did nothing to dispel this notion. After all, I did have influence on the universe of votes through bill scheduling and the positioning of amendments, and I occasionally would snag a needed vote by telling a recalcitrant Democrat, in my best stage whisper so others would hear, "This is a roll call vote for WEAC." This usually worked wonders, and I tried to foster a perception of my power regarding the legislative roll calls of other labor unions and farm and environmental groups.

Perhaps the secret weapon in WEAC's arsenal is the union's willingness to fight in primaries. The lower voter turnout in a primary will mean the votes of teachers and their families will count for more. Unfriendly incumbents, regardless of how "safe" they are in general elections (because their district is heavily Republican or Democratic), can easily be vulnerable in a primary election when facing an opponent backed by WEAC. WEAC is particularly strong in a primary where there is no incumbent. WEAC knows how to hunt where the ducks are. It also knows how to forge alliances to get what it wants. The case of Scott Jensen is a good example.

As Gov. Tommy Thompson's chief of staff, Scott Jensen was the administration's chief teacher baiter. This was not forgotten when Scott announced that he would be a candidate for the state Assembly in heavily Republican Waukesha County. A special election was being held after the governor appointed the incumbent to a judgeship. (Scott, a young man in a hurry to look back on a career he has yet to have, actually announced prior to the vacancy.) WEAC endorsed the other Republican in the primary, a farmer who did not believe in campaigning. It made a temporary alliance with the NRA and the pro-lifers, who did not believe Scott was pure enough on their issues. Scott's opponent made a very good showing even though he was outspent by thousands of dollars and restricted his campaign to the mailing of one piece of campaign literature. Scott squeaked by with only a forty-three-vote margin. For WEAC's reputation it was almost as good as winning.

UNIQUE POLITICAL INFLUENCE

The organizational structure and endorsement process lend polish to the advantages already built into the American political process for teachers, and for education. First, public education is a state responsibility; education policy and much of the money to implement it lie solely in the hands of the legislature. Thus, the races for the state legislature, and the partisan control of each house, are the main targets of the teachers' union, which pays little attention to congressional or municipal elections. This also means that the relatively big staff and big pot of campaign money controlled by the union can be targeted. No other interest group is quite so concentrated on legislative races. The teachers usually have the most chips and make the biggest bets, and because of this their odds of winning these contests are favorable.

Second, teachers are by definition opinion leaders. They certainly comprise the biggest group of college-educated people in most legislative districts. The teachers' union may be the villain to many, including newspaper editorial boards and big business, but the local teacher is still revered because education is America's secular religion.

My Aunt Eileen taught me American history in high school, and it certainly was her encouragement that fostered my interest in history and in politics. (She also suggested that I date a certain junior named Barbara Schasse who later became my wife.) My English teacher Joe Hostak, after reading an ungrammatical but lively essay, said, "I think you can write." This quite offhand praise, which I had never heard before, gave me the temerity years later to seek a job as a speech writer. And it was a miracle to me that one day I read a book to my son, and the next day he read a book to me. That day I was willing to put a plastic statue of his teacher on my dashboard.

INFLUENCE IN THE LEGISLATURE

As Morrie said many times, the legislature is WEAC's top priority because it can stop bad things from happening. The teachers' union has real power in the legislature, but it is not the queen on the chessboard.

After the legislature, the state's director of public instruction wields the most influence on issues the teachers' union cares about. This person interprets the rules that govern the day-to-day lives of teachers. The election for this nonpartisan post is held every four years in the spring. It's a low-interest, low-turnout race, which gives WEAC a great advantage. In fact, it would be big news if the candidate endorsed by WEAC lost.

Next comes the governor, who can also prevent bad things from happening through a friendly veto or two, and then comes the state supreme court. For example, the inherently unfair school funding formula in Wisconsin was upheld four to three by the court's conservatives, even though the same type of formula had been thrown out in other states, notably Kentucky. However, when deciding whether state tax money could be directed to private schools, the quartet of the status quo sang a different tune and said yes, this was allowed under Wisconsin's constitution. These were two bad decisions, and they were two big losses for WEAC, especially since its candidate had narrowly lost the last time one of the conservative judges was up for reelection. (Again a nonpartisan, low-turnout election in the spring.)

The WEAC endorsement is a curse in the governor's race, a partisan, high-turnout contest. When I ran for governor, it cost me more than it was worth. In a race as big and as intimately followed by voters as the gubernatorial contest, the WEAC organization and money are moved to the margin, and the millstone of the union weights one down. For example, I vividly remember my visit with the editorial board of the Wausau paper. I spent the whole time being grilled by six gentlemen about the teachers' union and defending its endorsement of my candidacy. (If I run for office again, I will pass on editorial boards and spend this time skipping flat stones on calm lakes and will probably gain the same result.)

Another incident from my race for governor illustrates WEAC's concentration on the legislature. It was clear Tommy Thompson was far ahead of me in some rural areas where there were tight legislative races. WEAC weighed in with a relatively accurate yet rather personal and negative barrage of attack ads. The ads criticized the governor for his flip flop on property taxes, but they were not meant to help me. They were designed to snip the governor's expected coattails in certain districts so the WEAC-endorsed candidates for the legislature would not be hurt.

WEAC hardly ever dabbles in local school board elections for the simple reason that there is a collective bargaining law. The school board has little real choice but to approve a contract negotiated through collective bargaining. It is the structure of the state bargaining law, not the friendliness or antagonism of certain school board members, that is important in this relationship.

SOPHISTICATED CAMPAIGN TECHNIQUES

WEAC's clout in campaigns does not come from the amount of money the union can give to a candidate. In a race for the state Assembly, a political action committee (PAC) can contribute a maximum of $500 to the candidate's campaign. This isn't very much, and since the total of all PAC contributions cannot legally exceed a modest limit, most candidates in targeted races will be "PAC'ed out" quickly. Thus, a PAC check from WEAC is the same value as that from any other group. PAC money is plentiful and fungible. Candidates who choose public funding cannot accept any PAC money, so they don't need the WEAC money at all.

WEAC's real clout begins with the volunteers who can be organized by the local political staff to help with literature drops, telephone banks, and mailings for an endorsed candidate. These activities are considered a legitimate part of the independent expenditure campaign waged by

WEAC and other PACs on behalf of a candidate. The law prohibits coordinating the candidate's campaign and a PAC's independent expenditure campaign, and the dividing line is not crossed for the law is enforced. (A similar process and ground rules exist in most states.)

The sophistication of WEAC's independent expenditure campaign on behalf of a candidate for the legislature depends on the closeness of the race. By definition, the marginal seats are close. Once again there tend to be few groups, other than the teachers' union, organized for campaigns in marginal districts because these races are usually in rural and suburban areas. The most effective albeit least sophisticated weapon in WEAC's arsenal of campaign techniques is the phone. Thirty local offices strategically located throughout the state are outfitted with phone banks. Twenty to thirty phones in each office are used to find and persuade voters, track down volunteers, and get out the vote for candidates in targeted races.

Another campaign technique that WEAC has mastered is the poll. In the mid-1980s WEAC took a giant leap and started to poll in individual legislative districts. A few years later it added tracking polls. This expensive but very accurate type of poll regularly tracks, usually every week, the candidate preferences of a large sample of likely voters in a targeted race. Tracking polls gave WEAC a weapon other groups simply did not have and could not afford. It was like the richest duke with the most fertile land also getting the first gunpowder army.

In contests between candidates of equal resources (which is what races in marginal areas have become), the winning candidate is often the one with the edge in knowledge of "how things are going." A poll can tell who's ahead and by how much. It also can tell who is undecided—the target group a campaign must focus on. Tracking polls enable WEAC to test different campaign themes and TV or radio ads, but their real benefit is to allow the union to shift resources from one front under control to another where reinforcements are needed, from a battle that is lost to a battle that can still be won.

Recently, WEAC has refined the focus group, allowing it to test potential tacks for going after an opponent or defending the endorsed candidate. A focus group is a representative sample of undecided voters. About twelve or fifteen people are gathered in a room and asked questions about issues or candidates. The questions are designed to help a campaign know what particular issue or candidate trait to emphasize or which way to twist the knife if the need is to "go negative." A focus group also is a way to test the effectiveness of ads and perhaps avoid spending big bucks to put a dud on the air. The focus group does not know that the firm doing the testing is a front. It is a way to "fast forward" a campaign to test the proposed strategy. The image of a psychiatrist in a white coat watching the behavior of dysfunctional patients through a two-way mirror would not be far afield. (It is a real B-movie scene when "people meters" are used; each subject twists dials to instantaneously register his or her likes and dislikes while watching a TV spot.)

District polling and the use of focus groups can really make a difference in a campaign. The best example occurred in what seemed to be Rep. Virgil Roberts's ninety-fifth consecutive tough race for the Assembly. Virgil had been a train dispatcher in La Crosse, and he ran for the Assembly four times before he was elected in 1970. He was reelected every two years in close contests, then lost in 1984 and regained the seat in 1986.

In 1990 it looked like Virgil was going down for the second time. His opponent was a Republican and a well-known local official. She was pro-life in a heavily Catholic district, and Virgil was pro-choice. However, polling and focus groups showed that if Virgil highlighted her position on abortion by concentrating on the fact that she did not support an exception for rape and incest, many voters would think her too harsh and out of touch. Soon TV ads attacking her position saturated the inexpensive La Crosse media market, and Virgil squeaked through. Only polling and focus groups, not instinct, experience, or example could have led to the decision to highlight the paradox of a pro-life candidate being too anti-abortion.

Campaign polling has evolved beyond the horse race question of "Who's winning?" WEAC and other interest groups now ask such questions as these: "When do the undecided make up their minds?" (the second week before the election). "Where do regular voters in legislative elections get their information?" (newspapers); "the sporadic voter?" (television). And, "How do voters react if an ad, especially a negative one, is sponsored by teachers?" (it depends).

There is no voter registration by party in Wisconsin, and there is no voter registration at all in communities of fewer than 5,000 people. WEAC has spent a lot of money to develop voter files in small communities. These lists, compiled from the handwritten lists kept by the clerk, are then checked by phone to find the Democrats, Republicans, and Independents. This information on party affiliation is then used in the independent expenditure campaigns in targeted races. These voter lists are expensive to develop and update, but they provide another edge that WEAC has and other interest groups do not.

LOCAL TEACHERS

To keep ties strong between the local teachers and the local legislator, and to build the personal relationships on which effective lobbying is based, WEAC does several things. As is often the case in life, intimate relationships start with dinner. Diplomacy also is best conducted over dinner. It is hard to be unfriendly to anyone you have shared a meal with. Therefore, WEAC invites area legislators and about 150 teachers to regular and timely dinners at a restaurant. The purpose of these mostly social occasions—there are cuddly speeches—is, in Morrie's words, "to build interest both ways."

When an important vote comes up in the legislature, WEAC's practice is to make sure that a teacher or two from the wavering legislator's district comes to the Capitol for a visit before the vote. This visitor from home will not be a stranger since the legislator will remember him or her from dinner, or from work as a volunteer on the campaign, or from something a mutual friend has said. Just as suspected, if a politician's former teachers are really needed, they are found.

Other WEAC tactics include letter-writing campaigns for a legislative candidate by local teachers from the candidate's district. A computerized system helps identify the teachers and generate the letters. It also puts out a political newsletter to the union representative in each school building in the state. If WEAC is concerned about how the legislature will handle a very important issue for teachers, it can summon to the Capitol a few thousand of its members. However, this is not the best tactic since several times the issue at hand was decided before they arrived or purposely delayed on the legislative calendar until long after the memory of WEAC's rally blurred with the memory of some other group's rally.

There is no big group, WEAC included, that can cry wolf on every vote it cares about. Gains come slowly, over several sessions, a bit at a time, and losses can sometimes be recouped in the other house of the legislature. According to Morrie, it is rarely wise to make an enemy or to burn any bridges. It is even better to make regular opponents of WEAC's legislation think they "owe one," rather than think they are on the outs with the union.

Of course, there are times when the stakes are high, and the vote is close. Then the faint must be propped up, and the double agents must be made to choose sides. This was the case with the early retirement bill and the ephemeral "yes" vote of Republican representative Randy Radtke, a former teacher.

THE PENSION FIGHT

Politicians who fool with the pensions of public employees learn what Pandora found out when she peeked in the box. The Wisconsin pension fund, which covers state employees and teachers, was flush with cash by the late 1980s from the bull market it had been riding, and it was time for an improvement in retirement benefits. It was also time for another "early retirement window." The window would be a two-year period when teachers and other public employees could choose to retire if they were at least age fifty-five, and if they met the "rule of eighty-five." (Their years of employment and their age had to add up to at least eighty-five.) The early retirement window had been opened before in Wisconsin. The older employees with the high salaries retired and were replaced by lower-salaried workers. The state and the school districts saved a lot of tax money in the switch, which also proved to be good for the system because the burned-out would choose to leave and the energetic and idealistic could enter. There wasn't a teacher, active or retired, in the state of Wisconsin who did not care about the fate of this pension bill.

Public employee pension funds are not for philanthropy, nor are they to finance the plans of others in the political arena. Politicians test this rule at their peril. To oppose the retirement bill, a group of ersatz tycoons was organized by the Wisconsin Manufacturers' Association into a coalition called STOP. This coalition, in addition to being clever with acronyms, could command the attention of the press, and it was representative of a force in the Republican Party akin to that of organized labor in the Democratic Party. STOP agreed the pension fund was flush, but it argued that this "dividend" should be returned to the taxpayers to compensate for the pension contributions the state and the local school districts made over the years on behalf of each of their employees. This line of reasoning made the teachers livid, especially the retirees, because it would "break open" the fund for a nonpension purpose. It also ignored the fact that the employer contribution was implicitly a part of a contract. The employer and the employee pension contribution shares were negotiated, and very often wage increases were traded away for increased pension contributions from the employer.

STOP and WEAC lobbed mortar rounds at each other in a war of attrition played out in the media. WEAC scored a hit by pulling its state convention out of Milwaukee; it did not want the 15,000 teachers at this annual meeting to spend their money in the town where the STOP leaders and their businesses were headquartered. WEAC also organized teachers to cancel their checking accounts and credit cards at a large bank whose president was a STOP member. This forced him to publicly quit the coalition. STOP could generate news but not votes in the legislature.

In the legislature the retirement legislation had more support than did resolutions praising motherhood. Well, perhaps not that much support, but the bill had plenty of votes in both parties so passing it wasn't the hard part. The fight was to get a two-thirds vote in each house to override Governor Thompson's expected veto and to do it before the 1987-88 session was scheduled to adjourn.

Big bills tend to ripen in the last days of a session, and it was near the very end of the final floor period that the first retirement bill had passed. It was then vetoed by the governor, who said "it went too far," meaning, we all presumed, that it had reached his desk. After the governor vetoed the first early retirement bill, he immediately presented the legislature with another similar bill—his bill. It seemed impossible that another bill could be maneuvered through both houses and onto his desk before it was time to adjourn. And this is what the governor was counting on. Nevertheless, the Democratic leadership teed up another bill. This bill was started in the Senate, so if the governor did veto it, which we did not think he could possibly do again, the override vote would first take place in the Senate, where the real fight seemed to be. The attempted override on the first bill had been four votes short in the Senate. The Assembly had another reason for having the Senate introduce the second bill. The Assembly felt it was the Senate's turn to host the WEAC lobbyists and the crowd of angry teachers.

THE GOVERNOR'S PENSION BILL

Within a week a version of this second bill was on the governor's desk. He vetoed it. It was late at night when we were told of the veto. I was in Majority Leader Tom Hauke's office, which is on the second floor just off the chamber. With Tom and me was David Clarenbach, the deputy Speaker, and we were waiting for my aide, Stephanie Case, to return from the governor's office with the veto message. Exhausted, we sat like zombies on Tom's green leather couches. We had kept our troops in session more than seven weeks past our originally scheduled date to adjourn. It was almost June of an election year. It was unusually hot, and the window was open. Beer was being consumed, and the mood was the chuck-it-all giddiness of the unrested. Stephanie returned with the news of another veto and said, with the exasperation of the still innocent, "You will not believe this. He gave us another retirement bill!" She held the bill, which was several inches thick and weighed in at two pounds. I said, "Throw it out the window." She did not, so I did. The big manila envelope sailed into the night and landed with a thud and a skid on the driveway below. David Clarenbach broke the silence when he stood up and thrust his fist into the air and yelled, "Yes!"

We decided to give up. We would stay until the Senate took a vote on the override and go into elections with the issue hanging. To keep awake on the drive home, I listened to the oldies station with the volume cranked up so far the speakers vibrated.

Solicitous of government property, Stephanie retrieved the bill after we had safely left. It had been run over, and there was a perfect impression of a black tire tread across its width. She joked the next day, "We should send it back to Tommy and say we are 'tired' of this bill."

To our delighted surprise, and theirs, the Senate voted to override the governor's veto, 23-8. So the showdown came down to the Assembly, and as expected some Republicans who had voted to override the first time, secure in the knowledge the Senate would not, switched their position. The WEAC tally sheet, which by this time was as accurate as a thermometer, indicated that the override was one vote short. The needed vote belonged to Randy Radtke, a Republican who had recently told some of his local teachers that he would vote to override, or so they thought.

THE DECIDING VOTE

The teachers thought Randy had told them he was on their side. The GOP, STOP, and the governor were privy to whispered assurances to the contrary. They confidently listed him as a "no" vote on their roll call. Well, as happens so often in vote counting, a "yes" became a "no." One day before the vote Randy met with four teachers from his district, a delegation that included his former high school English teacher. Randy had talked long enough, weaving and unraveling hypothetical voting scenarios, that the group left believing that his not saying "no" meant "yes." And Randy departed thinking that his not saying "yes" meant "no." I would imagine it was his former English teacher who felt possessed of the authority to pronounce Randy's rambling as a "yes." The word of this change (it meant the vote to override) spread among the teachers in his district faster than the news of school closing because of snow.

On the afternoon of the override vote, the Assembly chamber was packed with the same clans on each side of the question that had gathered all the other times the early retirement bill had been debated. There was little debate on the bill. It was a relaxed atmosphere. Regardless of the outcome of the override, we were out of there after the vote. Randy was not relaxed, however. In fact, he was trapped on the floor. Should he wander off in any direction, there awaited him a knot of teachers from his district, or a WEAC lobbyist, ready to pounce on him. Was he a "yes" as they believed? Or had he changed his mind, as they were now hearing? Randy was still not being real clear about what he had said the day before, and he was not putting the question to rest by sitting in his seat in the middle of the floor and staring straight ahead.

The Republican floor leader, Betty Jo Nelson, knew she had the votes. She was trying to quiet the firebrands on her side of the aisle who wanted to make the same old point yet again, which would inevitably provoke a response and prolong the debate. I was working on a way to allow Randy to kind of vote both ways with the effect being an override.

That day the total votes to work with could be reduced from ninety-nine (the number of members in the Assembly) to ninety-four. Two members were absent who could be "paired" with two members who were present, and one seat was vacant. A "pair" is an agreement between two members on opposite sides of a question not to vote on that question if one is absent. The absent member influences the outcome of that vote by, in effect, canceling the other vote. For example, if one of the ninety-nine members of the Assembly is absent, it still takes fifty votes to pass a bill (50+48=98). When that absent member voting "no" pairs with a member present, only forty-nine votes are needed (49+48=97).

My best-case tally, which included one secret Democrat who was willing to change and vote to override if it was "the vote," was sixty-two in favor of overriding and thirty-two (including Randy) against. This was one "no" vote too many for a two-thirds vote to override. I could reduce the "nays" to thirty-one by having Randy switch to a "yes" but pair with an absent Democrat who was voting "no." Since the present half of a pair abstains from voting, Randy would not actually vote in this scenario but by not voting he would be allowing the override. He could tell his teachers he voted "yes" and tell anyone else that he didn't vote.

Like a ten-year-old with a magnifying glass, a sunbeam, and a grasshopper, I focused the heat on Randy, carefully explaining this option to him in full view of WEAC and his local teachers. Once they grasped the scam, they of course thought this rather public duplicity the perfect out for Randy. (The records clerk, Ken Stigler, had worked out about a dozen combinations for me based on who I thought might change their vote or pair in an advantageous way at the last minute.)

Much to his credit, Randy stuck to what he had heard himself say all along and voted "no." My best-case roll call was off by one anyway, and the override failed (61-33), and we went home. Before we left the traditional gifts were given out to the leaders and the party caucus officers. Randy was given a T-shirt with a bull's-eye on the back.

WEAC felt it had to go after Randy in a big way, and as Morrie so delicately put it, "We got a candidate and went after him and spent a lot of money." Randy suffered but did not lose. Yet it was an effort that was talked about, and WEAC didn't lose because Randy won. Its reputation was enhanced, and years later when Randy thought about running for the state superintendent of public instruction, a post that would not be ill-served by his presence, he did not. It would have meant fighting the early retirement bill and explaining all over again, and all over the state, what he actually had said to his former English teacher.

10

Ethics and Lobbyists: A Scandal Worthy of the Name

I'm not a saint, but I'm not a mortal sinner.[1]

Lobbyist Gary Goyke

I would like to make it clear that, while I did cut corners, I never intended to violate the law.[2]

Former state senator Richard Shoemaker

This chapter presents a case study of an ethics scandal in the Wisconsin legislature, the only ethics scandal there in recent years. Given what I know of my colleagues in state legislatures throughout the country, I can say that it is easy to slide into the gray area of legislative life where lobbyists pick up the tab. This scenario is typical nationwide. However, small crimes elsewhere are big crimes in Wisconsin because of the state's historically high standards for political conduct. Wisconsin's "not even a cup of coffee" rule is atypical. In other words, lobbyists should not be plying legislators with booze, meals, cash, trips, or anything else, not even a cup of coffee. If an officeholder will accept a little corruption, he or she may accept more. Thus, even the smallest transgression carries with it a tough penalty.

Wisconsin's ethical standards, as expressed in its laws, are high. A legislator's income and debts are disclosed, and campaign contributors are listed by name and address. Wisconsin legislators are not better people or more ethical than others because of these tough laws. However, most have had the benefit of coming of age, going to school, and practicing

---

[1] *Wisconsin State Journal*, July 13, 1988.
[2] *Milwaukee Journal*, August 30, 1989.

politics in a state where the Progressives produced a culture of high expectations for politicians and government. The laws express the political history of the state, and the politicians are representative of this culture, the sweet fruit of generations of work in the political garden by reformers.

What is ethical and unethical under the law can be learned. Therefore, it should be taught. A state's legislature will be better off if the ethics laws are tough, and the inhabitants are schooled in the laws that govern their behavior. A state's political culture can be improved by spelling out in law the borders of acceptable behavior. A course of instruction giving a map of these borders should be required of all new members. But laws will not make saints out of mere mortals.

Ethical behavior is not what is legal versus what is illegal. Legal strictures cannot anticipate every possible human foible or temptation. Ethics are more like good table manners. There is no particular reward for them, but you know your mother would be pleased, and they make others at the table sit up a little straighter.

A PLACE OF TEMPTATIONS

The temptations in a legislature are far greater and more numerous than those in most other work places. Legislators' decisions can create monopolies, bail out failing enterprises, and make companies and individuals rich.

I never received an offer of a bribe (if you discount what is implicit in some campaign contributions). However, almost every enticement comes like a little whisper from the devil. You are presented with an opportunity to do something slightly wrong, not illegal, but a compromise in principle that would give you a silent partner with an I.O.U.

One day while the leadership was waiting for a tedious floor debate to die, my friend the minority leader, Tommy Thompson, buzzed me at the phone on the Speaker's rostrum. He told me that a chiropractor from Dane County had sent a will to him at his law office in Elroy. The man had told him to look his will over and send him a bill. The chiropractor's name was recognizable because he was usually the first to arrive at Republican and Democratic fundraisers. This happened a couple of days before we were to vote on a bill mandating that private insurers cover chiropractic visits, something the chiropractors had been fighting to have enacted for years. Tommy had always opposed this bill, but he was thinking of running for governor, and ambition was telling him to change his vote. Even if he continued to vote "no," he was the minority leader and could be of great help if he just blinked on one of the procedural moves needed to move the bill along. I said, "Send the will back and vote 'no.'" He did.

Sometimes a legislator is presented with a gift that may create an obligation even if it is refused. One day the mail brought a letter from a Wisconsin businessman who invited my wife and me to join him for a week of cruising in the Mediterranean off Greece on his yacht. Airline tickets would be held for me in Chicago if the date mentioned worked out. Some months earlier a lobbyist had introduced this man to me as someone who wanted to help in the Dukakis campaign in Wisconsin. The man had nothing pending before the legislature. I turned down the offer of joining him on his yacht. I didn't check, but I felt this offer must be illegal. And even if it wasn't, I would have felt guilty. Accepting the invitation would have been wrong even if it were not illegal. Furthermore, if the press had found out, I would have been pilloried. Just a few months later this gentleman became very interested in a bill before the legislature that, if passed with certain provisions, would have made him an even richer man. As it was, he certainly raised his visibility with me just by making the offer.

THE YOUNG, SMART LEGISLATORS

I came to the Wisconsin legislature in 1976 with a class of reformers determined to restore the public confidence in government shaken by Watergate. Led by Democratic governor Patrick J. Lucey, we passed the most sweeping changes in the way elections were conducted and government was operated since "Fighting" Bob LaFollette and the Progressives threw out the party bosses early in this century.

When the dust settled, Wisconsin had on the books public financing of campaigns, restrictions on contributions by political action committees (PACs), a tough ethics code administered by a nonpartisan watchdog board, an open meetings law for all governmental bodies, and an open records law that gave the public the right to see all government documents. Every one of these measures was a blow for freedom, with the open meetings and open records laws bringing real change, but our home run was election day voter registration. A person could walk in, show his or her driver's license, sign a registration card, and then be ushered by a clerk into the voting booth. We did not know of a place in the world where it was easier to vote or to run for office.

When I left the legislature at the end of 1990, Wisconsin had a new, even tougher ethics code, and the Dane County district attorney had just closed the books on the last of the legislators and lobbyists who had been involved in an influence-peddling scandal. It started with some of the young members.

Walter J. Kunicki was twenty-two when he was first elected to the Assembly in 1980 from Milwaukee's South side. He had just received his degree in occupational nursing from the University of Wisconsin at Milwaukee when he entered the Democratic primary and started to go door-to-door in the compact Twenty-Seventh District, a blue-collar and Hispanic neighborhood of bungalows huddled around the clock tower that rises above the Allen Bradley factory. Wally was local, likeable, Polish, and ambitious. The incumbent, Joe Czerwinski, decided not to seek reelection at about the time Wally hit the first door. Joe was past the stage in life when trying to outhustle an opponent held any appeal—especially if it was a young guy who thought knocking on doors was a great adventure. Joe knew what could happen because he was the nice young man at the door when he was elected in 1968 at age twenty-four. (Wally won the primary with 662 votes in a field of seven Democrats.)

Wally was on the rise the minute he hit the Capitol. If the Wisconsin legislature had a favorite nephew, it was Wally. He was always willing to help—to move things along, to get votes for the budget, to recruit candidates, and to raise money. In return he wanted to be given some responsibility so he could demonstrate his talent. His flaw was that he had yet to learn the difference between deal making and legislating.

My job was to make the place work and to give talent a chance and train future leaders. I appointed Wally to chair the Health Committee, where he did a good job, and then I moved him up the ladder to be a member of the Joint Finance Committee, where he proved a natural. At the start of the 1989 session, in a move that was necessary but not without risk, I made Wally the Assembly chair of the Joint Finance Committee. In this position he replaced the veteran Marlin Schneider. Marlin was honest and had a moral force that often prevented the Assembly from taking a wayward path, but he had a flip side. "Mr. Hyde" was prone to ill-tempered moralizing, and in this persona he couldn't make the committee work. Hyde was becoming dominant, making my job harder.

Wally expected me to make this switch. It was clear to me and to other veteran Democrats that Marlin needed to be removed, and Wally could sense this. Furthermore, although I didn't promise Wally the post, I led him to believe this would be the case if he took responsibility, with me, for the recruiting, hand-holding, and money raising needed to save our majority in the 1988 election. The election was something I was dreading because it was going to be a tough, expensive fight, and I was also going to be doing a double shift as the chair of the Dukakis campaign.

Thus, it was a remorseful young Walter Kunicki, the new chair of the Joint Finance Committee, who struggled to tell me of the soon-to-be-public ethics charge that he would face. He had invited me to Kosta's Restaurant, a legislative haunt, and over a Greek salad told me the story and said he was sorry. I sat opposite him, faced toward the window, and the harsh April sun made an undeserved halo appear above Wally's blond head. The lobbying scandal had been unfolding since July 1988. We had a budget bill to pass, and I was preparing to run for governor. Here was the kid I had bet part of the farm on, and he was trying to put the best face he could on this petty betrayal of his office. The news hit the papers shortly after our lunch.

> The Wisconsin Utilities Association was accused today of providing hotel rooms and $600 in meals for three Democratic legislators and the former Assembly sergeant at arms.
>
> The charges came as . . . [an investigation] into legislative lobbying practices was continuing in Dane County Circuit Court today, and came one day after Madison lobbyist Gary Goyke was charged with 12 felony counts of laundering campaign donations to hide that he was the source of the money.
>
> Named in the complaint as recipients of the association's largess were state Senator Richard Shoemaker, D-Menomonie, who is already facing criminal charges from the probe; state Rep. Walter Kunicki, D-Milwaukee. . . .
>
> Kunicki is co-chairman of the powerful Joint Finance Committee. . . .[3]

Wally had come far fast because of his talent and because of me. He had no leavening, but he had his mother's goodness in him, and I believed that his ambition—he was thinking ahead to running for Speaker—would help keep him on a straight path. By appointing him Finance chair the session I was going to leave, I had moved him to the starting line for the upcoming race for Speaker. Most chairs of the Joint Finance Committee had been considered automatic contenders when the Speaker's post opened up. This meant he would be watched carefully by his colleagues and the press. Why risk a bright future for a weekend on the town financed by a lobbyist? Wally admitted his transgression, paid his fine, and said he was sorry. I said nothing other than that I was disappointed. I did nothing more because in my career I had learned little from my critics. I had learned from my mistakes.

THE LEGISLATURE'S TOP LOBBYIST

Gary Goyke was a successful lobbyist with a six-figure income. As a former state senator, he had friends in all the right places, which, along with his genuinely nice personality, is why he rapidly rose from his defeat for reelection in 1982 to be the ace lobbyist of the legislature. By mid-1988 he had sixty-seven clients. In July of that year his world came crashing down. A magazine article revealed that good old Gary was relying on a little

---

[3] *Capital Times*, April 14, 1989.

more than his friends and good humor for access and influence. Like the great athlete who has it all and then risks it all by reaching for the steroids, Gary was looking for an edge and was doing a few favors for the legislature's favor seekers. He was good at granting favors because he made these petty grifters feel good about the perks he could provide. Gary's crowd enjoyed the game, the meal, and the drink a little better if they weren't paying. They were the ones whose smile had been replaced by a smirk after a couple of terms. They were also among the more talented and powerful members of the legislature.

Gary kept good records, like those a proud man might keep who expected them to be examined one day by his biographer. Gail Shiman, one of several lobbyists working for Gary in his growing firm and a former aide to the Senate majority leader, had photocopied receipts showing who was wined and dined by Gary. She copied these records to protect herself. In November 1987 Goyke suddenly fired her, intimating that some clients had complained about her work. She left town with the records, and she held onto them for a year. Then she apparently got nervous and decided to blow the whistle before someone else did. She knew that in politics this was done through the press. So she gave the records to a freelance reporter who once covered the capital, Paul Rix. He sold the juicy story for $4,000. The article was to appear in the August issue of *Milwaukee Magazine*, a glossy local publication usually read in waiting rooms.

News of the impending article on Goyke spread fast as Rix started to check facts and interview legislators he hinted were mentioned in Shiman's records. The rest of us had heard rumors galore, but as yet no one had seen the article or knew which legislators and lobbyists would actually be implicated. This was the first layer of the onion to be peeled away. It would take two and one-half years before the thing was ended, and the Dane County district attorney had made his last curious deal.

Gail Shiman was born on the fourth of July in 1941 in Knoxville, Tennessee. She was graduated from UCLA and went to graduate school in Vermont, where she served one term in the legislature in 1975. She came to Wisconsin with the Mondale campaign and stayed, camping out in the state Senate. Like rumble seats in the 1930s, she fit in with the times. For a person like Gail in a place like Wisconsin, the most exciting and glamorous place to be was with the young pols in the legislature. The heady days of fighting for right and cutting deals were followed at night by a round-robin of fundraisers with former colleagues turned lobbyists. Dinner usually capped off the camaraderie. If there was a battle cry for some in the state legislature in the 1980s, it was "dinner." The liquor was top shelf, and the food was good because somebody else paid.

LAUNDERING CAMPAIGN CHECKS

State and local investigators, galvanized by the news of the Goyke records involving legislators, did not wait for publication of the article. Shiman was worried about Goyke's unethical billing practices and the trouble she might get in because of them. (For example, he would pay a restaurant tab for a legislator and then submit it for reimbursement to a client as a lobbying expense.) The investigators were interested in something quite different when they took their first look at Shiman's records. Some of the documents clearly indicated that members of Goyke's staff were routinely reimbursed by Gary for campaign contributions given at his direction.

Shiman, and the other Goyke staffers, willingly participated in the laundering of campaign checks. It was part of the office procedure, and staff members were reimbursed by adding the amount of the campaign check to the "entertainment" category on their monthly expense account. Goyke would ask for a check from whoever was handy. ("Lucky, you weren't here. I was the only one around and had to write a check for Gary." [4]) Goyke would then deliver the check to a fundraiser he would attend, usually without a representative from any client in tow. It was important that the legislator see Gary Goyke at the fundraiser. The small check he dropped at the door, never more than $100, was a token.[5] It was Gary's appearance at the fundraiser that helped build a relationship between him and the legislator.

Never underestimate the ignorance of smart people concerning the rules that govern their activity. There is no doubt Goyke knew this laundering was against some rule somewhere, but I doubt if he knew it was a felony. There is not much evidence that Gail Shiman thought what she was doing was illegal. The whole staff wrote checks. It was just part of the stuff that lobbyists did. But Gary's "stuff" turned out to be more than penny ante, and the ensuing investigations turned up more rot.

A RACE TO THE NEWSPAPERS

Gary did not yet know what would be uncovered, since he didn't know what Shiman had and what she didn't have. But he did know, like most

---

[4] Wisconsin Department of Justice, Division of Criminal Investigation, Case Activity Report, interview with Brenda Gail Shiman, August 2, 1988. This quote is attributed to Goyke employee Ruth Ann Nelson by Shiman.

[5] The largest check Shiman wrote was for $100; most were for less than $50. The contributions went to members and candidates of both parties as well as to the parties themselves (for example, for admission to events such as the Democrats' Jefferson Jackson day dinner).

good politicians, to get his version of events into print quickly.

As a freshman in the state Senate almost a decade and a half earlier, Gary Goyke had led the fight against secrecy—against closed party caucuses, where the big decisions on the budget bill had always been made, and against the closed door meetings of the "Secret Seven." Seven Assembly Democratic members of the Joint Finance Committee would meet privately in the chairman's office before the committee meetings and work out the deals that would be perfunctorily ratified when the committee met officially.

Gary took his fight against the Secret Seven to the Wisconsin supreme court and won. He became the darling of the state press. It was no surprise then that his first instinct when he got into trouble as a lobbyist was to go to the editors and plead his case or, more accurately, put his spin on the story. He was also doing damage control with the members of the Wisconsin Newspaper Association, one of his major clients. By and large his strategy worked.

In the *Wisconsin State Journal* Goyke announced that he had called for an investigation of himself by the secretary of state. When asked if he had broken the lobby law, he replied, "I'm not a saint, but I'm not a mortal sinner." [6] The *Milwaukee Sentinel* ran the first of several complimentary profiles that appeared in the press. He was called "a superstar in influencing the legislature." [7]

When *Milwaukee Magazine* appeared, little was added to what was already known. The new news was that Goyke paid for a weekend at a Door County resort for Assembly Majority Leader Tom Hauke and his family. In addition, he was reimbursed by one of his clients, Pfizer Inc., for a pricey dinner at Morton's of Chicago for Richard Shoemaker, a state senator who at the time was a member of the Assembly.

The first cursory look into the activities of Gary Goyke quickly turned up the names of Shoemaker and big-time lobbyist Jim Hough. And just as quickly investigators found that Hough had also reimbursed his employees for writing out checks for campaign contributions.[8] Faced with a felony charge for laundering, Goyke cooperated and spilled his guts, putting the best face on his activities before investigators—thinking ahead, always working for his spin. The goal was survival as a lobbyist. Hough bled too, but he was granted immunity from further prosecution because the prosecutors wanted the scalp of a legislator. Even at this early stage they had

---

[6] *Wisconsin State Journal*, July 13, 1988.

[7] *Milwaukee Sentinel*, July 14, 1988.

[8] The list of laundered checks by Hough included one to my campaign committee for $75. *Capital Times*, April 8, 1989.

decided, wittingly or unwittingly, that violation of the law was more serious if done by a legislator than by a lobbyist. It was a bad decision.

"SHOE"

The Wisconsin Assembly was (and still is) a meritocracy that rewards talent early. Trying to hold self-confident and bright people down is like a swimmer trying to hold a beach ball under water. This way of operating is abetted by two things: seniority is not a factor in the election or appointment of legislators to a top job, and there is a timely, natural turnover of members that is helped greatly by reapportionment. So every session there are opportunities to run for leadership positions and for the Speaker to change the committee chairs.

State Rep. Dick Shoemaker ("Shoe") was talented. His colleagues sensed it the minute he walked in the place at the start of the 1981 session at age thirty. He would rise in the Assembly but not to the top. He would be the assistant majority leader (he fell one vote short of being elected majority leader), and he would be the chair of a major committee, but I would not name him to be the chair of the Finance Committee. In 1988, as the lobbying scandal was unfolding, he ran for an open seat in the state Senate and won.

Shoe gave credence to the cliché that appearance is everything. In fact, the volumes of documents accumulated by investigators detail, dinner by dinner and drink by drink, that the ones suspected of being the knife and fork crowd actually were the knife and fork crowd. The most organized group with its belly up to the bar and a napkin under its chin even had a name, the "Jobs Task Force." In Madison, Shoe was a regular at Namio's Restaurant. Dick Shoemaker was the patron Joe Namio dreamt about. He brought friends, ordered well (lamb chops were a favorite), and, after adding a nice tip, signed the bill—not with his name, however. On occasion, Shoe signed Gary Goyke's name, but usually he printed in big bold letters the name of lobbyist Jim Hough.[9]

The press sees the obvious, and capital reporters had a good read on Shoemaker, the elected official:

> The third of five children of Otto Shoemaker, a Menomonie mortician, and his wife Dona, Shoe is married and has two children. A former manager of a men's retail clothing store, Shoe always ranked among the

---

[9] Wisconsin Department of Justice, Division of Criminal Investigation, Case Activity Report, James E. Hough, May 3, 1989.

male legislator's sharpest dressers, favoring double-breasted suits and a panoply of colorful ties.[10]

> ... hard working, smokes, but doesn't drink. Family man. Natty dresser, but otherwise apparently modest lifestyle. [An] ... effective lawmaker who wins on controversial issues like gambling. Young successful politician with a sometime abrasive style, but not overly ambitious.[11]

Legislators viewed him a little differently than did the press. His colleagues liked him. I liked him. But he hung around with lobbyists and did little to dissuade you from the notion that he was somehow on the take. His manner said this arrogance should be excused and accepted because it was him. There is an arrogance that is charming, like Basil Rathbone's in the role of Sherlock Holmes, but this was not Shoemaker. He affected the role of the unrewarded, like the good but not great player who walks back to the huddle slowly in order to be noticed. His resigned look and burdened shoulders as he rose to leave when the session adjourned or the meeting ended seemed to say, "Where is the appreciation?"

Dick was also suspect because of the issues that he called "his"—the drinking, smoking, and gambling bills. These bills were "money" bills. A lot of campaign money could be raised by the chair of the committee with control of their fate. They were little bills that affected big corporations. For example, Phillip Morris cared a lot about the details of legislation to regulate smoking in public buildings. It was the chair who decided when the bills would have a hearing and when they might be sent to the Rules Committee to be scheduled for a vote. These bills were also called money bills because some business or some person would make money if they passed and, depending how they were written, just which business or person was also likely to be decided.

The gambling bills were the biggest money bills of the decade. On April 7, 1987, Wisconsin's constitution was changed to allow a state-run lottery and on-track pari-mutuel betting. (Many voters mistakenly believed the latter meant horse racing only.) The "yes" vote meant a jackpot for lobbyists. The groups wanting track licenses hired lobbyists to help influence the bill's language to give their proposed location an edge.

There followed a Darwinian fight for survival between the dog lobbyists and the horse lobbyists. If horse tracks were given a one-year lead time over dog tracks, a horse track not a dog track would get the most lucrative location—a track in the major population area running from Milwaukee to Chicago. If the legislation was silent on this point (which happened be-

---

[10] *Milwaukee Journal*, March 3, 1989.
[11] *Wisconsin State Journal*, March 5, 1989.

cause the governor vetoed the one-year head start for horse tracks), the dog tracks would win since their lower capital costs and lead time for construction meant they could be up and running quickly. There would not be enough gambling dollars for both a horse track and a dog track in any of the state's population centers.

INSIDE THE STATE AFFAIRS COMMITTEE

Shoe was in the saddle because he was the chairman of the State Affairs Committee, the committee with jurisdiction over the gambling bills. After Shoe failed to be elected majority leader for the 1988 session, I appointed him the chair of this committee because he was more than capable of the task, and this is what he requested. The State Affairs Committee was what he wanted, but it was a waste of his talent and experience. I tried to persuade him to become a member of the Joint Finance Committee, where his ability to master complex issues, his political knack, and his leadership experience would be of great benefit to the Assembly. I also wanted him on Finance so he would not have control of the upcoming gambling bills.

I was against gambling, especially gambling sanctioned and promoted by the state in order to raise tax revenue. This was un-Wisconsin, un-Lutheran, un-Progressive, and I didn't care if I was unenlightened and unrepresentative about what the voters wanted. I railed at the proposed lottery, calling it a "tax on stupidity" (generating several letters from citizens claiming they were not stupid). But when the referendum won handily, it was my job to make sure we ended up with a good lottery law and tight regulation of racing.

My distaste for state-promoted gambling was such that I couldn't participate in writing this law or even reading the competing proposals. So I proceeded to do what Speakers are supposed to do, and I set up a process that would result in a decent bill being passed. To produce a good bill and one that wasn't totally written by lobbyists, I diffused the responsibility for making the decisions among several players. This would spread out the lobbyists so they couldn't concentrate solely on the State Affairs Committee, and it would limit Shoe's ability as the chair to make unilateral decisions on a subject never before considered by the legislature.

A SAFEGUARD COMMITTEE

To deal with the pari-mutuel issue, I introduced on April 28, 1987, a resolution calling for the creation of a Select Committee on the Regulation of

Gambling. The need for it was obvious. No one had any experience in crafting such a law, and we would only get one shot at it. The resolution passed the same day, and I appointed Rep. Dismas Becker as the chair and peppered the membership with some liberal do-gooders. "Dis" was not a member of the knife and fork crowd, and he was the least likely to succumb to persuasion by the fast assembling gang of track speculators and lobbyists who saw this bill as their meal ticket for this session and sessions to come.

I put Tom Hauke on the committee because he could lip-read an offer of untoward favor mouthed from around a corner. Shoemaker was an automatic. He had to be in at this stage because he would eventually have the bill in his committee and be the one to report the likely final version to the floor. Without any reluctance, the committee agreed to run around the country visiting tracks to find out what other states had done wrong and what they had done right. I hoped they would then be able to counter the one-sided view they were certain to hear at home. Gambling was being promoted as jobs, a source of painless tax revenue, and as a way to fund every future scheme ever to grace a press release. In the vernacular of the terminally redundant, it was a "win, win" situation.

Two nights after the special gambling committee was set up, Shoe dined at Namio's with two guests, probably Assembly colleagues. He had lamb chops; the bill, with $36.15 in drinks and a 20 percent tip, came to $132.49. As he had been doing since August 1985 (and would continue to do until May 1988, when he started to feel the heat of the investigation), Shoe signed Jim Hough's name to the tab.[12]

THE "HIRED GUN"

Hough later told investigators that he recalled receiving through the mail "groups of bills from Namio's that Shoemaker had accumulated from approximately the previous month." He admitted that he billed some of his clients for the meals. The choice of which clients to bill "was totally arbitrary."[13]

Jim Hough didn't care who he billed because, like Goyke, Hough's influence needed to be personal. To be a big-league contract lobbyist, you had to have a reputation for being able to get things done. This, in turn, hinged on being a pal to those legislators in the right places to wield influence on a number of issues. If you could reduce this crowd to a few

---

[12] Receipts attached to Case Activity Report, James E. Hough, March 27, 1989.
[13] Case Activity Report, James E. Hough, March 27, 1989.

well-placed people, it was easier to be influential. If a little cash on the side helped, well, hell, a black Lincoln and a house in the Highlands eased the conscience. Besides, in any other state but Wisconsin, this stuff wouldn't be that illegal. But Hough wasn't just another guy getting his, cutting a few corners along the way.

Hough was a mercenary, a hired gun. Yes, he was a friend to Shoemaker and others, but more like Iago to Othello than Huck Finn to Tom Sawyer. He fed Shoemaker's self-destructive tendencies (figuratively and literally). It's hard to find a reason for Hough's risks. He was already successful, and rich by Wisconsin's low standards and the standards of his peers. Evil is a mystery. It would have been easy for Hough to say "no" to Shoemaker, who still would have carried large pails of water for Hough's clients. Hough said "yes" because this was how he played the game.

It was no mystery why Hough had friends in the legislature. He started out as the lobbyist for the Wisconsin Bar Association and parlayed his good reputation earned with that establishment group into a successful contract lobbying business. Hough could walk into a room in such a deferential way that it appeared he was actually backing out. His manner was like the medieval church official who counsels the prince that the contemplated treachery is within bounds because there are certain laws, even church laws, that the prince is above. Like the prince, the legislators who were Hough's friends could take his self-serving counsel (and his American Express card) and still feel superior.

THE UNWRITTEN RULES

The prosecutor said at the end of the affair, "No votes were bought." He missed the point. In a legislature things are traded; it isn't necessary to make money on every deal. Whether things are traded inside or outside of the rules determines the ethics of a legislature.

It's not the relationship between the favor, the client, and the pending vote that counts. It's the relationship between the legislator and the lobbyist. Accumulating these personal chits for favors led to easier access, more influence, more clients, a higher billing rate, and more friendly looks when the lobbyist walked in the room. Like hired guns, lobbyists live by their reputations. The prosecutors were confused when they failed to find even one vote that had been bought. They didn't know the rules, and by letting Goyke and Hough continue to lobby, though Goyke paid a high price, they missed their chance to improve the ethics of the place.

A WIRETAP

Other leads on Shoemaker resulted from Goyke's chatty talks with investigators. He told them that "Shoemaker had a close and strange relationship with lobbyist Tom Dohm."[15] Indeed he did. Dohm gave Shoemaker money because Shoe thought of asking him for it.

Starting in early 1986 and ending with a $1,000 check in September 1988, six weeks after the ethics scandal had hit the newspapers, Dohm gave Shoemaker a total of $4,620.50. Shoemaker was cadging cash by defrauding his campaign committee, and he was dining on the tabs of Goyke and Hough, making a little profit, but his other racket was to just get money from his friend Tom Dohm.

Tom Dohm got nothing for this. He wasn't a player. I would not know him if he were standing next to me today, although I certainly must have met him or talked to him. His two groups, the Wisconsin Property Taxpayers' Association and Wisconsin Independent Businesses, more or less existed to solicit members and collect dues. Looking for cash opportunities, Shoemaker asked Dohm for money one day, and he gave it to him. Dohm said he wanted to help him out because they were friends and had been friends before Dohm became a lobbyist. When asked by investigators, Dohm could not come up with one piece of legislation that he was trying to influence.

When the investigators listened to the one-party wiretap Dohm agreed to, they heard two guys that were pretty ignorant of the ethics and lobby laws. For some reason, Shoe thought that if they could argue the checks were loans, it might be legal to accept them since the total amount of the checks was less that $10,000. On the first couple of checks, they had put items on the memo portion of the check—for example, snowblower, desk—so it would seem the money was for purchases Dohm made from Shoemaker. Soon, however, they had dropped even that faint subterfuge. Shoe seemed amazed his bank would make copies of checks he deposited ("I can't imagine that they make photostatics of these checks. . . .") Neither of them knew much about what was happening to them, but it was clear from some of their wiretapped conversations that they were indeed friends.

---

[15] Wisconsin Department of Justice, Division of Criminal Investigation, Case Activity Report, interview with Gary R. Goyke, February 1, 1989. In this and other interviews Gary talks freely about the rumored sins of others and fingers Tom Dohm. He also admits reimbursing his employees for campaign contributions when they attended fundraisers, a felony.

DOHM: I don't even know how a John Doe [investigation] works, do you?
SHOEMAKER: I don't either. . . . I really don't.
DOHM: I don't know if they . . . put you under oath or if . . . they say okay what are these [checks] for and I say they were loans and they say okay did he pay them back.
SHOEMAKER: . . . there's going to be some problems with that, but . . . I'll argue that we have a right to do that and that they were short term . . . and that it was a cash flow problem for me . . . let it fall down on me there . . . because they've got enough unanswerable questions on me. . . .
DOHM: Yeah, okay. Well Shoe wish me luck. . . .
SHOEMAKER: Yeah, well, get to a lawyer Tom. . . . People like me come and go but you gotta make your living [lobbying in Madison].[16]

Despite admitting reimbursing employees for campaign contributions, the crime that would make Goyke a felon, Dohm was given immunity from criminal charges. However, he ended up not figuring in the Shoemaker case at all. The charges relating to the cash payments—Dohm giving, and Shoemaker soliciting—were dropped because Dohm could not testify under oath that he asked for or expected anything in return for the money. The Wisconsin law didn't contemplate a lobbyist giving a legislator money and asking nothing in return.

THE MAJORITY LEADER IS CHARGED

While the investigators tied up the cases against Shoemaker, Goyke, and Hough, the press pursued Majority Leader Tom Hauke. More press attention was devoted to Tom than to any other story in the ethics saga, mainly because he didn't admit guilt, fought the charge, feigned no remorse, and, worst of all, tried to change the ethics law by introducing a bill.

Unlike Goyke, Hauke wouldn't play the victim. Unlike Hough, he wouldn't shut up. He was like a staggered boxer who refused to go down. Although the punches and cuts by the press produced buckets of political blood, his attitude remained, "Hit me 'till you drop."

For the press the Hauke case was a "no brainer" and no work because Tom basically wrote the story. The capital press received no reward for original work or even uncovering scandal. They were given no incentive, time, or budget to investigate anything. The business-minded editors made them watchdogs without teeth. The reporters were there to cover events. That's all their editors asked for, and that's all they did.

---

[16] Wisconsin Department of Justice, Division of Criminal Investigation, interview with Thomas D. Dohm, October 24, 1988, attached wiretap transcript.

The *Milwaukee Magazine* reported that Gary Goyke paid the $168 hotel bill for Tom Hauke and his family's weekend stay (May 24 and 25, 1986) at Bailey's Harbor Yacht Club in Door County. New England-like Door County is the thumb-shaped peninsula that sticks out into Lake Michigan from Green Bay. Goyke was the lobbyist for the commercial fishermen along Lake Michigan, and he had asked Hauke several times to visit and go out on one of their boats. Hauke said he assumed his host, a commercial fisherman, paid for the weekend, and that he had no idea Goyke had picked up the tab.

The incident is the only transgression by Hauke that came up or was even rumored during the whole two-year-plus affair. In a preemptive move Hauke hired an attorney to investigate "the facts surrounding the payment of the two nights lodging." It didn't take a clairvoyant to guess how Hauke's attorney would interpret what happened. To Hauke the attorney wrote:

> It is clear that without your knowledge, lodging at the Bailey's Harbor Yacht Club was paid for by Mr. Goyke [American Express]. It is also clear that you have unknowingly and unintentionally violated the Wisconsin Statute regarding the receipt of anything of value by an elected official from a lobbyist.[17]

HAUKE FIGHTS THE PRESS

Hauke stuck to this story and said, in effect, "If you think I knew Goyke paid, prove it." On November 14, 1988, just after the election, the state's Ethics Board filed a civil complaint against Hauke accusing him of using his official position to obtain the Bailey's Harbor weekend, and it sought the maximum fine of $1,500. Hauke quickly announced he would fight the charge. The next day the *Capital Times* stated in an editorial that Hauke should not run for reelection to the post of majority leader because of the "taint" of the pending ethics case. ("What kind of message will the Democrats send to the citizens of this state if they honor someone as their leader who is caught in the net of the expanding legislator-lobbyist inquiry?") Two days later Hauke was easily reelected majority leader in the Democratic caucus, fending off a credible challenge from a veteran legislator. I voted for Hauke.

The big news was that Hauke would fight the charges. For some reason the press portrayed this as being wrong—ethically wrong:

---

[17] Letter to Tom Hauke from Attorney Michael J. Jassak, Habush, Habush & Davis, South Carolina, July 20, 1988.

"Hauke to contest charges."
"Hauke disputes ethics charges."
"Hauke didn't ask who paid."
"At the very least, it's very poor judgement." [18]

These stories were followed a couple of days later with headlines expressing the press's incredulity that Hauke had been reelected to his leadership post. ("Despite ethics charges, Hauke is named leader."[19]) Somehow the rest of us were looked upon as unethical because we had reelected Hauke majority leader, a job he had performed brilliantly, in our view, for the past two years.

Hauke did make it easy for the press to pummel him, and he showed no fear (perhaps the real rub). Like someone throwing raw meat just outside the reach of a chained dog that was used to being petted and fed well, Tom taunted the press as best he could. He called for an audit of the "leaderless" Ethics Board, which he said was "running amok." [20] After his court appearance (on the stand he proved more than a match for the special prosecutor), he told the press, "My constituents couldn't care less. . . . I'd do it again tomorrow." [21] Then he took the gloves off.

Hauke said his trip to Bailey's Harbor was fact-finding and a legitimate part of his job. The prosecutor said it was a family vacation that Hauke had solicited from a lobbyist. The press agreed with the prosecutor. The war was on. Hauke's hometown paper declared,"Ethics defense insults citizens." [22] Hauke had this to say to the *Milwaukee Journal*: "There's only one thing worse than living in a country with a censored press and that is living in a country with a free press that . . . tries to deny the truth." [23] "Freeloading Hauke should step down," commented the *Capital Times*.[24]

The end came fifteen months later on February 16, 1990. A judge ruled that the ethics law, in the case of a civil violation, did not require prosecutors to prove that Hauke knew that Goyke paid the Yacht Club bill. The fact that Goyke had paid was enough. The judge said it was elected officials' responsibility to find out who was picking up their bills.

[18] *Milwaukee Journal*, November 15, 1988; *Capital Times*, November 15, 1988; *Capital Times*, November 16, 1988; and *Milwaukee Journal*, November 17, 1988.
[19] *Milwaukee Journal*, November 17, 1988.
[20] *Wisconsin State Journal*, December 13, 1988.
[21] *Milwaukee Journal*, December 14, 1988.
[22] *West Allis Star*, December 28, 1988.
[23] *Milwaukee Journal*, January 25, 1989.
[24] *Capital Times*, February 23, 1989.

Hauke, having appealed at every step, had exhausted his appeal opportunities. He finally paid the $1,418 fine.

Hauke was arrogant in the eyes of the press because he did not act like a politician. During this time he also introduced a bill to change the ethics code. The press suggested that he had somehow forfeited this right that all legislators have because, in their view, he was at the symbolic center of the ethics controversy. The fault lay in him. His hometown paper finally called for his resignation. He would not repent. He ran for reelection to the legislature in 1990 and won easily. Despite the certainty he would be reelected majority leader, Tom ran for Speaker (an open position because of my departure). He told me he wanted to give it a try because this would be his last term. The Democratic caucus chose Wally Kunicki instead for Speaker.

After months of bargaining between his lawyer and the prosecutor, Shoemaker agreed to plead guilty to five misdemeanors and to resign and serve a ninety-day jail term in his home county. Five felony charges were dropped. Goyke was given a choice of a felony conviction on the laundering charges, which would not carry with it a loss of his lobbying privileges, or a misdemeanor conviction, which, as part of the deal, would prohibit him from lobbying for eighteen months. Goyke chose to become a felon in order to continue lobbying. Hough paid a fine and was barred from lobbying for six months.

LESSONS

Ethical behavior in a legislature is fostered by tough laws, leaders who set an example, fear of the press, and penalties that fit and that are consistently applied. All are necessary to hold up the ethics of the institution, like the four legs supporting a chair.

Fear of the press is essential for a good ethical climate in a legislature. It is a deterrent. For the press to be effective in this watchdog role, legislators, staff, and lobbyists must believe their untoward actions have a reasonable chance of being exposed. The thud of the newspaper on the doorstep should make the politician's heart beat a little faster.

Fear of the press is also important because elections are not the place where good ethics are rewarded or bad ethics punished. All of the legislators who were caught for ethical misconduct in Wisconsin won reelection except one; he lost for other reasons.

When I was first elected, members of the legislature feared the press. For example, the *Capital Times* was a true crusading paper with a mission to hold politicians to the highest standard. Many a time, safely behind closed doors, I saw a dubious move that was contemplated dropped like a hot rock when someone would say, "If we did that, the *Capital Times* would crucify us."

Later in my tenure the newspapers started to confuse criticism of the legislature with investigative journalism. They were either at a politician's feet, lavishing praise, or at the throat, heaping scorn, and they ceased to strike fear because of it.

INCONSISTENT PENALTIES

It was hard for legislators and citizens to follow the legal course of the investigations in the Wisconsin scandal. The penalties paid by the legislators were negotiated and decided out of court—the result of behind-the-scene logrolling and bargaining by prosecutors and lawyers for the legislators and lobbyists. Hough's penalty was the same as that given to former state senator Carl Otte, a very minor figure in the scandal; as a lobbyist working for Goyke, Otte had bought a few meals for old friends.

The penalties were inconsistent, and it was obvious the prosecutors, especially the Dane County district attorney, saw the charges against the lobbyists mainly as levers to get at legislators. When the prosecutors couldn't find what they thought they would find—vote buying—they lost interest in the lobbyists. However, the ethical climate of the legislature would have been better if Hough had paid a real penalty. Were the crimes of Goyke greater than Hough's? Only in the eyes of the prosecutors. The goal was to get Shoemaker out of the legislature, not to get the bad actors out of the lobbying game.

The prosecutors held Hough until last. There was one more nasty detail in the scandal to clear up, and Hough was at the center of it. The prosecutors were counting on him to give them the proof they needed to remove state senator Barbara Ulichny from office. Hough had implicated her, saying that his financial favors to her were solicited by her administrative assistant. But the more Ulichny's former aide (and boyfriend) talked, and he talked a lot, the worse Hough looked. This didn't do the prosecutors any good because Hough had been given immunity from most things early on. He would get an easy fate for his fawning cooperation.

The announcement that Ulichny would not be tried, only fined for civil misdemeanors, was a surprise. The breathless press coverage had seemed to be leading up to something big. (Prosecutors fed the ravenous press with details of a train trip Ulichny took with her aide and Hough's American Express card.) Instead, felony charges were dropped, and Ulichny pleaded guilty to civil violations of the ethics code for accepting meals, basketball tickets, and Amtrak tickets from a lobbyist.

LEADERS

I asked Shoemaker into my office one day to ask him point-blank about a rumor. Had a lobbyist (one who was never above suspicion) paid for some electrical work on his house? He said, "No, it's not true. Honest, Tom. But I know why there are these rumors about me." He was looking out the window toward Lake Mendota, and the North light made him squint. His shoulders were heavy, and he smoked a cigarette. I asked him another time about a different rumor. We were in the hall behind the chamber that led to my office, and my aide Stephanie Case was there and could hear us. Again, he said, "No, it wasn't true." I didn't ask him a third time (perhaps fearing something Biblical would happen).

What would I have done if Shoemaker had admitted the rumors were true? Was it my job as Speaker to police my colleagues? I don't think so. When an Ethics Committee, or some other disciplinary body in a legislature, tries to punish the conduct of wayward members, the debate invariably becomes partisan. Furthermore, the nature of partisan leadership is to protect party members. I vividly remember what happened when a legislator was accused of soliciting an off-duty policeman for sexual favors in a park near his home. Party leaders quickly found a place with a religious-sounding name where he could be sent to hide and claim to be recovering from "stress." And they did other things to soften the impact this incident might have on his reelection. An outside body, like an independent Ethics Board, with the ability and budget to investigate at its own initiative, is the best method of enforcement.

Leaders are responsible for setting an example. I thought I knew where to draw the line in order to set an example. I knew the rules and didn't dance near the edges. In hindsight I should have had a policy that would have been a deterrent. But thinking of all the levers that were mine to pull as Speaker (such as appointments and bill referrals), I can think of none designed to deter unethical behavior.

The leaders of a legislature should make sure their behavior—especially their behind-the-scenes behavior—is well within the bounds of the law and common sense. A leader who is real chummy with lobbyists should realize that it is noticed. The appearance is wrong, and some legislators will conclude that this is the way the big boys act.

The raw meat Tom Hauke provided the press gives insight into the general legislature bashing that goes on in the press. The supposedly innocent are not to act arrogant. And it is politicians' arrogance, not just their misdeeds, that has invited the bashing. As much as I admire Tom, he should have thought more like a politician and less like the tough lawyer that he is. The legislature would have been better off. Being not guilty is not the same as being innocent in politics. Too much bad has happened to expect the press to come to the legislature without a jaundiced eye. A leader owes the institution the appearance of propriety. He or she will then get the benefit of a doubt when something goes wrong.

LOBBYISTS AND FORMER COLLEAGUES

"Mr. Speaker, I ask unanimous consent that a piano be rolled onto the Assembly floor. A whore house this ornate shouldn't be without one." I said this during my first term. I was losing my fight against a heavily lobbied bill, and I felt my colleagues were "selling out" to the flock of lobbyists who had gathered to join in on this raid on the treasury. My whore house comment was not well received because it reflected a stereotypical view of the relationship between lobbyists and legislators that was not true.

In reality this bill was being pushed by the governor, and it had a lot of voter clout behind it. The fight was well publicized, and everyone was watching everyone else. The lobbyists were simply representing their groups or interests. Less visible bills, the ones that affect only a few and benefit them greatly, are usually the ones that test the moral fiber of lobbyists and legislators.

The relationship between legislators and lobbyists often is based on friendship. Your seatmate one session may walk in as a lobbyist the next session. Shortly after his defeat for reelection to the state senate, Carl Otte started to lobby on the Goyke team (the designated lunch-buyer position), and he continued to share the apartment he had always shared with Rep. Virgil Roberts. Why not? They had roomed together after Virgil lost his Assembly seat some years earlier and lobbied for the railroads until he was reelected.

Former colleagues, of either party, are the best lobbyists because they have instant access and know the rules and the issues. A legislator-turned-lobbyist of either party could get in to see me without an appointment—at least the first time—and had more credibility with me than the slickest "government relations" vice president from a big corporation.

Three of my former administrative assistants left my employ to become lobbyists. Needless to say, their influence came from their comfortable access to me, the Speaker, as well as from their access to legislators on both sides of the aisle and in both houses and to the governor. They thought nothing of hanging out at their old desks, using the phone, leaving their coats and briefcases in our care, and failing to put a quarter in the kitty for their coffee. They had a status that excused them from this toll that was theoretically required of drop-ins of their ilk.

The easiest lobbyists to deal with and the ones most important to the system are those who represent large groups with broad interests, like labor, business, or local governments. Ed Johnson, who was the lobbyist for the Wisconsin League of Municipalities, was *the professional*. More than understanding the process, he cared about the state and patiently brought to each new member of the legislature a sense of the historical relationship between the state and local governments.

Ed had a tough nut to crack in me. I thought I knew what the relationship should be, and I wasn't very appreciative of the compromises that had been made over the years to produce the current arrangement. Besides, in my first reelection bid, ninety out of ninety-three local officials in my district endorsed my opponent. I won reelection handily, but the episode did nothing to endear me to the issues the local officials cared about. But Ed waited me out, repeatedly pointing out that the mayor of my hometown at least had the good sense to remain neutral. Over the years I moved toward Ed's view of things quite a bit, and he moved toward my view of things not a lick. He, and there were others like him, made the place work as much as the legislators themselves.

Shortly before Ed Johnson retired, after thirty years with the League of Municipalities, he came into my office and said, "Finally, now we can go golfing, and I can buy you lunch." When he retired a second time from lobbying, this time for the University of Wisconsin-Madison faculty, he came to me and volunteered to help in my race for governor and handed me a $500 check for my campaign. I was surprised and humbled. (Two quite rare feelings by this point in my political career.) It was only then, after all the years, did I know his politics. And it wasn't clear that he was a Democrat. He had always seemed to walk in his own path, a route partisans like me couldn't locate on the map. Ed believed in government and his responsibility to do his part right.

There is no legal stricture to govern the relationship between legislator and lobbyist, and even the things your mother taught you don't help.

Dismas Becker was my colleague and friend. On my office wall hung a photo of him with blood streaming down his cheek and across his priest's collar. It was taken years before when he was a protester at the capitol. After he lost his race for the state Senate, he became a lobbyist (for the trial lawyers!).

In the Assembly "Dis" had fought by my side and had supported my bills. He baptized my son Alec. Next thing I knew he was a lobbyist, sitting in my office asking me to help him help his client. What do you do? This is the same person that stuck with you through thick and thin, so if you are me, you help if you can. You stay within the rules, but Dis gets an edge because he is a friend and you are thinking, "There but for the grace of God go I."

The relationship, however, changes. The legislator and the former colleague no longer have the same agendas. If you are the legislator, your friend is now being paid to see you on behalf of a special interest. And how much money he or she makes often depends on the coziness of the relationship and your position in the legislature.

Legislatures Then and Now

Between 1977, my first year as a member of the Wisconsin legislature, and 1990, when I ran for governor, I witnessed many institutional and personal changes in state government. In this concluding chapter I review some of those changes and assess their significance.

A legislature can be an institution where individuals act collectively for the public good. A legislature can also be a cesspool of individualism. Unfortunately, the latter describes many state legislatures in recent times. I will not say that individualism has been the sole reason for scandal, gridlock, public disgust, and the popularity of term limits, but it is a monster that will destroy the community that is a legislature.

ALL FOR ONE OR ONE FOR ALL?

There are always some in office who think of themselves as a legislature of one, rather than one member of the legislature. This certainly should not be a surprise. Strong and ambitious individuals who can tout personal accomplishments are prized by Americans and are damn good candidates for office. Once in office, however, they must become part of a collective process of compromise. It is not altruism that works this transformation. It is the rules and mores of the legislature that harness these individuals and eventually make them pull in the same direction. And it is loyalty to party.

Rep. Tom Hauke was no hero. He fought the ethics charge against him like the tough guy he was. But he could not see that as the majority leader he owed his colleagues a quieter fight. His actions hurt his party. He expected his party members to understand his need for support, but he did not understand their need, and the need of the legislature, for him to box in the shadows so the public would not think us all arrogant crooks.

166

When the rules, the leaders of the legislature, the public, the press, and the party tolerate too much individual power, the interests of the individual members quickly dominate, and the good of the community takes a back seat. Once the community is weakened, the strong tend to become warlords. The Speaker or minority leader or chair of a powerful committee can become warlords because the center is weak and because they can extract money from interest groups and individuals who need to do business with them.

The reaction to the "all for one" attitude of powerful members has been predictable and healthy. Several states have enacted term limits. In California the initiative referendum has brought not only term limits but also restrictions on the size of the staff and the budget of the legislature. In addition to term limits, Colorado now has new rules, imposed by referendum, governing party caucuses. Their purpose is to prevent Democrats or Republicans in the House or Senate to put forward a "party" position on legislation.

I said the reaction is healthy. After all, the philosophy of the founders was that power must be restrained and balanced. The political process must be designed to bring forth "representative" officeholders who are then able to produce results representative of the will of the people. Term limits, a crude way to dislodge the influence of political money, may also foster the founders' goals. But by themselves they will not bring about much real change. They are based on the mistaken notion that if only the right individuals were elected, all would go well. (I would argue that if only we had stronger parties, things would go better.) But, alas, those who swoon over a good-looking process will find their love unrequited. A 100 percent turnout on election day in a publicly funded race for the legislature between Moses and Solomon would not bring forth the dawn of a new day even if there were similar candidates in every district.

CATALYSTS FOR CHANGE

Change in legislatures comes from a switch in party control, new leaders, a new governor, the rejuvenating effect of reapportionment (new voters will make an old legislator learn new tricks), and new members. The election of more minority members was a fundamental change wrought by reapportionment. This made legislators more representative of American society. The election of women legislators in significant numbers has meant great change in legislatures, and it was brought about by society.

When I was the assistant to the Speaker in 1975, I saw him place the name of a woman on the list to be one of the Assembly members of the Joint Finance Committee. This would have been a first. Her name was

Midge Miller. Just before the public announcement of this list of committee members, the other Democratic members of the Finance Committee stormed into the Speaker's office, and I witnessed their vociferous protest. "It will be harder to cut deals!" they cried. "Will she meet in secret?" If she wouldn't meet in secret, how could the "compromises necessary to pass a budget" ever be hammered out? "The caucus won't accept this!" Standing in front of the Speaker's desk, these gentlemen went on and on. Almost a captive, the Speaker sat there listening to their near shouts about how Midge just wouldn't do. In the end he backed down.

In 1983, my first term as Speaker, I decided to appoint Mary Lou Munts to be the Assembly chair of the Joint Finance Committee, the second most powerful position in the Assembly. She would be the first woman to chair this powerful committee. Her appointment was thought a risk on my part, and I, too, was confronted by friends who warned, "The caucus won't accept this!" If there was a refrain that was typical, it was, "I hope you know what you are doing." The accompanying look said, "I wash my hands of this. You are on your own, pal."

Both Midge and Mary Lou were liberals, and this was part of the charge against them, but men who were even more liberal who had been appointed were not questioned. Furthermore, ours was a caucus dominated by liberals. I had quietly asked advice of some, but I knew enough not to ask for consent. I had the good sense to hold my cards close to my chest on this decision, and I presented it as a done deal. As I expected, she was great in the job.

In 1993, during Wally Kunicki's first term as Speaker, he appointed a woman to chair the Joint Finance Committee. Rep. Barbara Linton was only starting her third term, and she had no experience on the committee or in budget matters. She was not from Madison or Milwaukee but from so far North that Lake Superior was a boundary of her district. No one blinked an eye. In fact, Wally would have had some explaining to do if he had not picked a woman chair. His problem was to choose between the many qualified women legislators in the caucus, all of whom were in the hunt for power.

The place changed because of the increase in the number of women members. Suffice it to say that the debate, the coalitions, the issues considered all changed for the better. It is already the case that in legislatures around the country women hold powerful posts, including that of Speaker, and this trend will continue. These women will bump up in the system and increasingly become candidates for governor and the U.S. Congress.

Caucus campaign committees, which strive to retain or gain majority-party status in a house of the legislature, have brought changes for the better in state legislatures. And this is not only because they have increased competition between the two parties, which is a good in and of itself.

This election-oriented party within a party within the legislature has made the inhabitants of state legislatures think more in terms of party responsibility and somewhat less about individual aggrandizement. The concept of retaining, or not losing, the majority, or gaining the majority, is understood by the members. The leaders press for an agenda and try to pass things that will give their caucus members "something to run on." The minority leaders press their members for a serious alternative—something that says, in effect, "If we were in the majority, this is what we would do."

A REAPPORTIONMENT DANGER

Can there be too much representation? The rules of reapportionment require that African American voters essentially be guaranteed that they can elect an African American candidate to the state legislature in areas where they are concentrated. This applies almost exclusively to the urban core of large cities. Milwaukee is a good example because it has the most segregated housing pattern of any large city in America.

Milwaukee has a ghetto. The concentration of the African American population, which is mostly poor, is so great in the central city that reapportionment for the 1992 elections produced five such Assembly districts. In each district an African American was assured of election. Each assembly district must draw a line around approximately 50,000 people. And voters in each of the five districts elected an African American.

To make sure that an African American candidate can be elected, the courts allow a legislature to add more African Americans to a district to compensate for low voter turnout and low voter registration. (Because the ghetto population is relatively young, fewer people are of voting age.) Each of the five Milwaukee Assembly districts mentioned above has an African American population exceeding 65 percent.

If there is any question about the difference in voting turnout in African American districts versus others, one need only look at the November 1990 general election in Wisconsin. In the three Milwaukee central city Assembly districts, all represented by African Americans, the total vote for Assembly candidates was a little over 14,000. In my old district and the two comparable adjoining districts in Dane County, the total turnout was almost 51,000.

The reapportionment rules stem from federal court rulings outlawing prevailing practices that were used to limit the representation of African

Americans in legislatures and in Congress. Until the 1970s it was common for state legislatures to "pack" African Americans into a single district to limit their representation in the legislature to perhaps one member. Or legislatures would divide up the African American population to make sure it was always a small voting percentage of a legislative district. This ensured that whites had a comfortable voting majority, and no African American candidates would ever be elected.

As they have evolved, the reapportionment rules have brought us back to "packing." Packing was abetted by a movement that emerged during the 1991 reapportionment fights around the country. Some African American incumbents in state legislatures, all Democrats, joined with some Republicans in a movement to concentrate even more African Americans in central city districts. The African American legislators, to put the best spin on their motives, wanted to "pack" legislative districts so the real election choice would be between two African American candidates. The Republicans were not duplicitous and clearly stated that by aiding in this strategy, they stood to gain if urban whites ended up being pushed into districts dominated by suburban voters, who were presumably Republican voters.

So what is the problem? The problem is that there is now political gain to be made from making sure ghettos remain and even grow in population. Politicians, if allowed, let alone encouraged, by the courts, will not willingly pursue policies that tend to destroy their voting base. This is not devious, or even intentional; it is just natural.

For example, many proposals are debated in the Wisconsin legislature to make life in the central city of Milwaukee better. A great deal is said about school choice, more police to fight crime, more clinics, enterprise zones, job training, and so on. It is good that this debate takes place. However, there are no real complimentary proposals designed to break the segregated housing pattern. It is instructive to observe that the issue debated is whether the state should provide vouchers for poor kids to attend better schools outside the central city, rather than a debate over whether to give parents housing vouchers that would allow them to move to places where there are better schools and more jobs available.

MORE REPRESENTATIVE GOVERNMENT

So some things are better in state legislatures, and some things are not as good as they could be. On balance, however, the representation test is better met in state legislatures now than it was a decade ago. The people are more representative in age, occupation, race, and gender. I can't judge whether Edmund Burke's test—representatives who both represent *and* employ "mature judgement"—is better met now, but this seems to be a cyclical thing anyway.

If there is one good thing to say in conclusion about state legislatures, it is that they are still a place where the journey toward a better place—the idea of America—is believed in and embarked upon daily. I loved my fourteen years in the legislature, and I am still very much in awe of the institution as the embodiment of representative democracy.

Index

DATE DUE
